HEINEMANN MODULAR MATHEMATICS
for
EDEXCEL AS AND A-LEVEL
Revise for Pure Mathematics 1

Michael Kenwood

Edexcel
Success through qualifications

Heinemann Educational Publishers,
Halley Court, Jordan Hill, Oxford OX2 8EJ
Part of Harcourt Education

Heinemann is the registered trademark of Harcourt Education Limited

First published 2001

05   04   03

10   9   8   7   6   5   4

ISBN 0 435 51110 6

Cover design by Gecko Limited

Original design by Geoffrey Wadsley; additional design work by Jim Turner

Typeset and illustrated by Tech-Set Limited, Gateshead, Tyne and Wear

Printed in the United Kingdom by Scotprint

Acknowledgements:

The publisher's and author's thanks are due to Edexcel for permission to
reproduce questions from past examination papers. These are marked with an [E].
  The author also wishes to thank Geoff Mannall for all his care, patience and
generous help in reading the proofs, making many useful suggestions and
checking the answers.
  The answers have been provided by the author and are not the responsibility
of the examining board.

About this book

This book is designed to help you get your best possible grade in your Pure Mathematics 1 examination. The author is a former Principal examiner and has a good understanding of Edexcel's requirements.

Revise for Pure Maths 1 covers the key topics that are tested in the Pure Maths 1 exam paper. You can use this book to help you revise at the end of your course, or you can use it throughout your course alongside the course textbook *Heinemann Modular Mathematics for Edexcel AS and A-level Pure Mathematics 1* which provides complete coverage of the syllabus.

Helping you prepare for your exam

To help you prepare, each topic offers you:

- **Key points to remember** – summarise the mathematical ideas you need to know and be able to use.

- **Worked examples and examination questions** – help you understand and remember important methods, and show you how to set out your answers clearly.

- **Revision exercises** – help you practise using important methods to solve problems. The questions and examples are at exam level so you can be sure you are reaching the right standard, and answers are given at the back of the book so you can assess your progress.

- **Test yourself questions** – help you see where you need extra revision and practice. If you do need extra help they show you where to look in the *Heinemann Modular Mathematics for Edexcel AS and A-level Pure Mathematics 1* textbook.

Exam practice and advice on revising

Examination style paper – this paper at the end of the book provides a set of questions of examination standard. It gives you an opportunity to practise taking a complete exam before you meet the real thing. The answers are given at the back of the book.

How to revise – for advice on revising before the exam, read the **How to revise** section on the next page.

How to revise using this book

Making the best use of your revision time

The topics in this book have been arranged in a logical sequence so you can work your way through them from beginning to end. But **how** you work on them depends on how much time there is between now and your examination.

If you have plenty of time before the exam then you can **work through each topic in turn**, covering the key points and worked examples before doing the revision exercises and Test yourself questions.

If you are short of time then you can **work through the Test yourself sections first**, to help you see which topics you need to do further work on.

However much time you have to revise, make sure you break your revision into short blocks of about 40 minutes, separated by five- or ten-minute breaks. Nobody can study effectively for hours without a break.

Using the Test yourself sections

Each Test yourself section provides a set of key questions. Try each question:

- If you can do it and get the correct answer then move on to the next topic. Come back to this topic later to consolidate your knowledge and understanding by working through the key points, worked examples and revision exercises.

- If you cannot do the question, or get an incorrect answer or part answer, then work through the key points, worked examples and revision exercises before trying the Test yourself questions again. If you need more help, the cross-references beside each Test yourself question show you where to find relevant information in the *Heinemann Modular Mathematics for Edexcel AS and A-level Pure Mathematics 1* textbook.

Reviewing the key points

Most of the key points are straightforward ideas that you can learn: try to understand each one. Imagine explaining each idea to a friend in your own words, and say it out loud as you do so. This is a better way of making the ideas stick than just reading them silently from the page.

As you work through the book, remember to go back over key points from earlier topics at least once a week. This will help you to remember them in the exam.

Algebra

1

Key points to remember

1 Laws of indices:
$$x^a \times x^b = x^{a+b}$$
$$(x^a)^b = x^{ab}$$
$$x^a \div x^b = x^{a-b}$$
$$x^0 = 1$$
$$x^{-a} = \frac{1}{x^a}$$
$$x^{\frac{1}{a}} = \sqrt[a]{x}$$
$$x^{\frac{a}{b}} = \sqrt[b]{x^a}$$

2 Rationalising the denominator:
$$\frac{1}{\sqrt{a}} = \frac{1}{\sqrt{a}} \times \frac{\sqrt{a}}{\sqrt{a}} = \frac{\sqrt{a}}{a}$$
$$\frac{1}{a+\sqrt{b}} = \frac{1}{a+\sqrt{b}} \times \frac{a-\sqrt{b}}{a-\sqrt{b}} = \frac{a-\sqrt{b}}{a^2-b}$$
$$\frac{1}{a-\sqrt{b}} = \frac{1}{a-\sqrt{b}} \times \frac{a+\sqrt{b}}{a+\sqrt{b}} = \frac{a+\sqrt{b}}{a^2-b}$$

3 To add or subtract polynomials, add or subtract corresponding terms.

4 To multiply two polynomials, multiply each term of the first by each term of the second and then collect like terms.

5 Factorising polynomials:
$$x^2 + 2xy + y^2 \equiv (x+y)^2$$
$$x^2 - 2xy + y^2 \equiv (x-y)^2$$
$$x^2 - y^2 \equiv (x-y)(x+y)$$
$$x^3 + 3x^2y + 3xy^2 + y^3 \equiv (x+y)^3$$
$$x^3 - 3x^2y + 3xy^2 - y^3 \equiv (x-y)^3$$
$$ax + ay \equiv a(x+y)$$
$$x^2 + (a+b)x + ab \equiv (x+a)(x+b)$$
$$acx^2 + (ad+bc)x + bd \equiv (ax+b)(cx+d)$$

6 To find constant coefficients in an identity:
    (i) equate the coefficients of corresponding terms
or (ii) give the variable specific values.

7 To divide one polynomial into another, use long division.

8 The factor theorem:
If $f(x)$ is a polynomial and $f(a) = 0$, then $x - a$ is a factor of $f(x)$.

Also if $f(x)$ is a polynomial and $f\left(\dfrac{b}{a}\right) = 0$ then $(ax - b)$ is a factor of $f(x)$.

9 Quadratic functions:
$b^2 - 4ac$ is the **discriminant** of $ax^2 + bx + c$

The graph of $y = ax^2 + bx + c$ is a parabola that:
- cuts the x-axis twice if $b^2 - 4ac > 0$
- touches the x-axis once if $b^2 - 4ac = 0$
- misses the x-axis if $b^2 - 4ac < 0$
- has shape ⋂ if $a < 0$
- has shape ⋃ if $a > 0$

$a < 0, b^2 > 4ac$

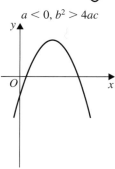

$a < 0, b^2 = 4ac$

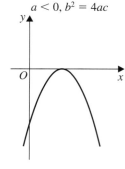

$a < 0, b^2 < 4ac$

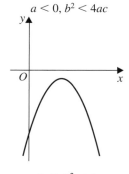

$a > 0, b^2 > 4ac$

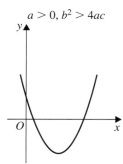

$a > 0, b^2 = 4ac$

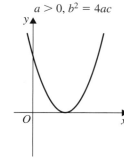

$a > 0, b^2 < 4ac$

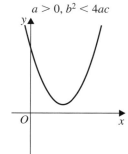

10 To solve a quadratic equation $ax^2 + bx + c = 0$
either:
- factorise

or
- complete the square

or
- use the **quadratic formula**
$$x = \frac{-b \pm \sqrt{(b^2 - 4ac)}}{2a}$$

11 To solve simultaneously one linear and one quadratic equation in x and y:
(i)   make either x or y the subject of the linear equation
(ii) substitute this into the quadratic equation
(iii) solve the resulting quadratic equation.

12 Inequalities:
$>$ is greater than
$\geqslant$ is greater than or equal to
$<$ is less than
$\leqslant$ is less than or equal to

If $x > y$ then:
$$x \pm c > y \pm c$$
$$mx > my \quad \text{if } m > 0$$
$$\frac{x}{m} > \frac{y}{m} \quad \text{if } m > 0$$
$$nx < ny \quad \text{if } n < 0$$
$$\frac{x}{n} < \frac{y}{n} \quad \text{if } n < 0$$

To solve a quadratic inequality $f(x) > 0$:
(i) find the **critical values** where $f(x) = 0$
(ii) draw up a table showing the sign of $f(x)$ in each of the regions of the graph of $y = f(x)$, between each two consecutive critical values, between $-\infty$ and the first critical value and between the last critical value and $+\infty$.

Example 1

Given that $p = 3^{-\frac{1}{3}}$, find the value of:

(a) p^6

(b) $\dfrac{1}{p^3} - p^3$

Answer

(a) $p^6 = (3^{-\frac{1}{3}})^6 = 3^{-2}$

$\qquad\qquad = \dfrac{1}{3^2}$

$\qquad\qquad = \frac{1}{9}$

(b) $\dfrac{1}{p^3} - p^3 = p^{-3} - p^3$

$\qquad\qquad = (3^{-\frac{1}{3}})^{-3} - (3^{-\frac{1}{3}})^3$

$\qquad\qquad = 3^1 - 3^{-1}$

$\qquad\qquad = 3 - \frac{1}{3}$

$\qquad\qquad = 2\frac{2}{3}$

> Using $(x^a)^b = x^{ab}$ from **1**

> Using $x^{-a} = \dfrac{1}{x^a}$ from **1**

> Using $x^{-a} = \dfrac{1}{x^a}$ from **1**

> Using $(x^a)^b = x^{ab}$ from **1**

> Using $x^{-a} = \dfrac{1}{x^a}$ from **1**

Example 2

Given that $p = \sqrt{5} + \sqrt{3}$ and $q = \sqrt{5} - \sqrt{3}$, prove that:

$$\frac{2}{p} + \frac{2}{q} = p + q$$

Answer

$$\frac{2}{p} + \frac{2}{q} = \frac{2}{\sqrt{5} + \sqrt{3}} + \frac{2}{\sqrt{5} - \sqrt{3}}$$

$$= \left(\frac{2}{\sqrt{5} + \sqrt{3}} \times \frac{\sqrt{5} - \sqrt{3}}{\sqrt{5} - \sqrt{3}}\right) + \left(\frac{2}{\sqrt{5} - \sqrt{3}} \times \frac{\sqrt{5} + \sqrt{3}}{\sqrt{5} + \sqrt{3}}\right)$$

$$= \frac{2\sqrt{5} - 2\sqrt{3} + 2\sqrt{5} + 2\sqrt{3}}{5 - 3}$$

$$= \frac{2(\sqrt{5} + \sqrt{3}) + 2(\sqrt{5} - \sqrt{3})}{2}$$

$$= \frac{2p + 2q}{2} = p + q$$

> Using **2**

> Using $(x - y)(x + y) \equiv x^2 - y^2$ from **5**

Worked examination question 1

(a) Prove that

$$(1 + x + x^2)(1 - x + x^2) \equiv 1 + x^2 + x^4$$

(b) By taking $x = 10$ and using the identity in (a), find the prime factors of 10 101.

Answer

(a) $(1 + x + x^2)(1 - x + x^2) = 1(1 - x + x^2) + x(1 - x + x^2) + x^2(1 - x + x^2)$

$$= 1 - x + x^2 + x - x^2 + x^3 + x^2 - x^3 + x^4$$

$$= 1 + x^2 + x^4$$

> Using **4**

(b) When $x = 10$, $1 + x^2 + x^4 = 1 + 100 + 10\,000 = 10\,101$

When $x = 10$, $(1 + x + x^2)(1 - x + x^2)$

$$= (1 + 10 + 100)(1 - 10 + 100)$$

$$= 111 \times 91 = 3 \times 37 \times 13 \times 7$$

The prime factors of 10 101 are 3, 7, 13, 37.

Example 3

Factorise $6y^2 - y - 15$

Answer

$acy^2 + (ad + bc)y + bd \equiv (ay + b)(cy + d)$

So $bd = -15$, $ac = 6$ and $ad + bc = -1$

If $a = 3$, $c = 2$ and $b = -5$, $d = 3$

then $ad + bc = (3 \times 3) + (-5 \times 2) = -1$

So $6y^2 - y - 15 = (3y - 5)(2y + 3)$

> Using **5**

> To give $ac = 6$ and $bd = -15$

Example 4

Divide $(x^3 - 13x - 12)$ by $(x + 3)$

Answer

$$
\begin{array}{r}
x^2 - 3x - 4 \\
x + 3{\overline{\smash{)}\,}} x^3 + 0x^2 - 13x - 12 \\
\underline{x^3 + 3x^2} \\
-3x^2 - 13x \\
\underline{-3x^2 - 9x} \\
-4x - 12 \\
\underline{-4x - 12}
\end{array}
$$

Multiply $x + 3$ by x^2

Subtract and copy $-13x$

Multiply $x + 3$ by $-3x$

Subtract and copy -12

Multiply $x + 3$ by -4

Example 5

Find the constants A, B and C such that:
$$A(2x + 3)^2 + B(2x + 1)(2x + 3) + C(2x + 1) \equiv 10x + 9$$

Answer

Let $x = -\frac{3}{2}$:

So that $2x + 3 = 0$

$$
\begin{aligned}
A(0)^2 + B(-2)(0) + C(-2) &= -15 + 9 \\
-2C &= -6 \\
C &= 3
\end{aligned}
$$

Let $x = -\frac{1}{2}$:

So that $2x + 1 = 0$

$$
\begin{aligned}
A(2)^2 + B(0)(2) + C(0) &= -5 + 9 \\
4A &= 4 \\
A &= 1
\end{aligned}
$$

Compare coefficients of x^0:

Put $x = 0$

$$9A + 3B + C = 9$$

Substituting $A = 1$, $C = 3$ gives:

$$
\begin{aligned}
9 + 3B + 3 &= 9 \\
3B &= -3 \\
B &= -1
\end{aligned}
$$

Worked examination question 2

Given that $f(x) \equiv x^3 + kx - 12$ has a factor $(x + 3)$, find the value of k.

Answer

If $(x + 3)$ is a factor of $f(x)$ then $f(-3) = 0$

Using **8**

$$
\begin{aligned}
\text{So} \quad (-3)^3 - 3k - 12 &= 0 \\
-27 - 3k - 12 &= 0 \\
-3k &= 39 \\
k &= -13
\end{aligned}
$$

Example 6
Complete the square:
(a) $x^2 + 6x + 13$
(b) $-5x^2 + 6x - 7$

Answer
(a) $x^2 + 6x + 13$

Find half the coefficient of x and square it. Add and then subtract it.

$x^2 + 6x + 13 + 3^2 - 3^2$
$= (x+3)^2 + 13 - 3^2$
$= (x+3)^2 + 4$

> Using $x^2 + 2xy + y^2 \equiv (x+y)^2$ from $\boxed{5}$

(b) $-5x^2 + 6x - 7 = -5\left(x^2 - \dfrac{6x}{5} + \dfrac{7}{5}\right)$

> Taking out a factor of -5

Find half the coefficient of x and square it. Add and then subtract it.

$-5\left(x^2 - \tfrac{6}{5}x + \tfrac{7}{5}\right) = -5\left[x^2 - \tfrac{6}{5}x + \tfrac{7}{5} + \left(-\tfrac{3}{5}\right)^2 - \left(-\tfrac{3}{5}\right)^2\right]$

$\qquad\qquad = -5\left[x^2 - \tfrac{6}{5}x + \left(-\tfrac{3}{5}\right)^2 + \tfrac{7}{5} - \tfrac{9}{25}\right]$

$\qquad\qquad = -5\left[\left(x - \tfrac{3}{5}\right)^2 + \tfrac{35}{25} - \tfrac{9}{25}\right]$

$\qquad\qquad = -5\left[\left(x - \tfrac{3}{5}\right)^2 + \tfrac{26}{25}\right]$

> Using $x^2 - 2xy + y^2 \equiv (x-y)^2$ from $\boxed{5}$

Example 7
Solve the equation $x^2 - 5x + 2 = 0$

Answer
If $x^2 - 5x + 2 = 0$

then $x = \dfrac{5 \pm \sqrt{(25 - 4 \times 1 \times 2)}}{2}$

$\quad = \dfrac{-5 \pm \sqrt{17}}{2}$

$\quad = \dfrac{-5 \pm 4.123}{2}$

$\quad = \dfrac{-9.123}{2}$ or $\dfrac{0.876\ldots}{2}$

$\quad = -4.56$ or -0.438

> Using the quadratic formula from $\boxed{10}$

Example 8
Find the set of values of x for which $5x^2 + 3x \leqslant 14$

Answer

$$5x^2 + 3x - 14 \leqslant 0$$
$$(5x - 7)(x + 2) \leqslant 0$$

Writing all the terms on the LHS

The critical values occur where $(5x - 7)(x + 2) = 0$

Using **12**

The critical values are $x = \frac{7}{5}$ and $x = -2$

These divide the graph of $y = 5x^2 + 3x - 14$ into the regions where $x < -2$, $-2 < x < \frac{7}{5}$ and $x > \frac{7}{5}$

Draw up a table to show the signs of $(5x - 7)(x + 2)$ in these regions:

x	$x < -2$	$-2 < x < \frac{7}{5}$	$x > \frac{7}{5}$
$5x - 7$	$-$ve	$-$ve	$+$ve
$x + 2$	$-$ve	$+$ve	$+$ve
$(5x - 7)(x + 2)$	$+$ve	$-$ve	$+$ve

So

$$5x^2 + 3x - 4 = (5x - 7)(x + 2) \leqslant 0$$

for all values in the set $-2 \leqslant x \leqslant \frac{7}{5}$

Worked examination question 3
Solve the equations:

$$3x + y = 1 \qquad \text{①}$$
$$x^2 + y^2 = 4x + y \qquad \text{②}$$

Answer

From ① $y = 1 - 3x$

Using **11**

Substituting in ② gives

$$x^2 + (1 - 3x)^2 = 4x + (1 - 3x)$$
$$x^2 + 1 - 6x + 9x^2 = 4x + 1 - 3x$$

Using $(x - y)^2 \equiv x^2 - 2xy + y^2$ from **5**

$$10x^2 - 7x = 0$$
$$x(10x - 7) = 0$$

Using $ax + ay = a(x + y)$ from **5**

$$x = 0 \text{ or } \frac{7}{10}$$

When $x = 0$, $y = 1$

When $x = \frac{7}{10}$, $y = 1 - \frac{21}{10} = -\frac{11}{10}$

The solutions are $(0, 1)$ and $\left(\frac{7}{10}, -\frac{11}{10}\right)$

Revision exercise 1

1. Given that $p = \sqrt{3}$ and $q = \sqrt{2}$, evaluate:
$$(2p - q)^2 + (p + 2q)^2$$

2. Evaluate $3\sqrt{45} - \sqrt{20} + \sqrt{245}$, giving your answer in terms of $\sqrt{5}$.

3. Sketch, on separate diagrams, the graphs of the functions:
   (a) $y = x^2 + 4x + 4$
   (b) $y = x^2 - 4x - 4$
   (c) $y = -4 + x - x^2$
   Mark on your sketches the coordinates of any points where a curve meets the coordinate axes.

4. (a) Solve the equation $4x^2 + 4x - 9 = 0$, giving the roots to 2 decimal places.
   (b) Find the value of k for which the roots of the equation
$$x^2 + 7x + k = 0$$
   are equal.

5. The triangle ABC has $AB = (2\sqrt{2} + \sqrt{3})\,\text{cm}$, $BC = (2\sqrt{3} - \sqrt{2})\,\text{cm}$ and $\angle ABC = 90°$.
   Calculate:
   (a) the area of $\triangle ABC$
   (b) the length of AC.

6. $E \equiv (x - 3y)^2 - x(x - 6y) + 2$
   (a) Prove that E is independent of x.
   (b) Find the least value of E and the value of y for which this occurs.

7. Given that $x^2 + y^2 = 23$
$$xy = 1$$
   and by considering an appropriate identity, find the possible values of $x + y$.
   Find the positive value of $x - y$ in surd form.

8. Factorise $4x^2 + 29x + 7$.
   By choosing an appropriate value of x, find two integer factors of 42 907, neither of which is 1 or 42 907 itself.

9. Factorise completely:
   (a) $(2x + 1)(x + 2) - x$
   (b) $(3x + 1)^2 - (1 - 2x)^2$

10 Find the set of values of x for which:

(a) $x - \dfrac{x-1}{3} < 1$

(b) $(2x+1)^2 < (x-3)^2$

11 Solve the simultaneous equations:

(a) $(x+y)^2 = 4$
$\quad 2y - x = 0$

(b) $5x - y = 17$
$\quad\quad xy = 12$

12 m and n are negative constants such that:
$$(m - \sqrt{3})(1 + n\sqrt{3}) = 5\sqrt{3} - 7$$
Find the exact values of m and n.

13 Given that $p = 2^{\frac{1}{3}} - 1$, $q = 2^{\frac{1}{3}} + 1$

(a) find the value of pq

(b) prove that $p^2 q + pq^2 = 4 - 2^{\frac{4}{3}}$

14 By considering a right-angled isosceles triangle, or otherwise, show that
$$\cos 45° = \sin 45° = \tfrac{1}{2}\sqrt{2}$$
Hence express
$$\frac{1 + 2\sin 45°}{5\cos 45° - 2\sin 45°}$$
in the form $a + b\sqrt{2}$ where the constants a and b are to be found.

15 Given that $\quad (\sqrt{5} - 2)A = 3 + \sqrt{5}$
and $\quad\quad\quad (9 - 4\sqrt{5})B = \sqrt{5} - 2$
find both A and B in the form $p + q\sqrt{5}$, and state the rational numbers p and q for each case.
Hence show that $A - 5B = 1$.

16 Find the exact square roots of $11 + 2\sqrt{30}$ in surd form.

17 Find, to 2 decimal places, the roots of the equation
$$x - \frac{2}{x} = \frac{2}{5}$$

18 Solve for x and y the simultaneous equations:
$$3x + 2y = 1$$
$$x^2 + y^2 = 4x + 2y$$

19 $f(x) \equiv x^3 - 7x^2 + px + q$

Given that $f(x)$ is divisible by $(x - 2)$ and by $(x + 3)$, find the values of p and q.

Find the third factor of $f(x)$ when the other factors are $(x - 2)$ and $(x + 3)$.

20 **(a)** Solve the simultaneous equations:
$$3y - 5x = 6$$
$$y^2 - 3x^2 = 22$$

(b) Solve for t, the equation:
$$4^{3t-1} = 16^{1-t}$$

21 **(a)** Given that $p = 125$, find the values of:

(i) $p^{-\frac{1}{3}}$

(ii) $p^0 - p^{-\frac{2}{3}}$

(b) Solve the simultaneous equations:
$$2^x = 4^y$$
$$3^{x+2} = 9^{3y-1}$$

Test yourself	What to review
	If your answer is incorrect:
1 Solve the equation $x^2 - 8x - 10 = 0$, giving your answers in surd form.	*Review Heinemann Book P1 pages 39–40*
2 Given that $p = \sqrt{3}$ and $q = \sqrt{2}$ prove that $\dfrac{1}{p - q} = p + q$	*Review Heinemann Book P1 page 4*
3 Given that $x - 2$ is a factor of $3x^2 - x - k$, find the value of k and the other factor of this polynomial.	*Review Heinemann Book P1 pages 27–29*
4 Factorise $10x^2 + 19x + 6$.	*Review Heinemann Book P1 pages 10–13*
5 Find the set of values of x for which $x^2 - 4x \geqslant 12$	*Review Heinemann Book P1 pages 42–46*
6 Solve the simultaneous equations: $x^2 + y^2 = 25$ $x - y = 1$	*Review Heinemann Book P1 pages 41–42*

7 Given that
$$1 + 2x - 2x^2 \equiv B - 2(x + A)^2$$
find the values of A and B.
Hence deduce the maximum value of $1 + 2x - 2x^2$
as x varies.

Review Heinemann Book P1 pages 14–21

---

8 Express $x^2 + 6x + 10$ in the form
$$(x + A)^2 + B$$
and find the constants A and B.
Hence prove that:
$$0 < \frac{1}{x^2 + 6x + 10} \leqslant 1$$

Review Heinemann Book P1 pages 32–36

---

9 Given that $p = 125$, find the value of $p^{\frac{2}{3}}$.

Review Heinemann Book P1 pages 1–2

---

10 Divide $x^3 + 5x^2 + 11x + 10$ by $x + 2$.

Review Heinemann Book P1 pages 21–26

Test yourself answers

1 $x = 4 \pm \sqrt{26}$ **3** $k = 10, 3x + 5$ **4** $(2x + 3)(5x + 2)$ **5** $x \leqslant -2, x \geqslant 6$ **6** $(-3, -4), (4, 3)$ **7** $A = -\frac{1}{2}, B = 1\frac{1}{2}$, max is $1\frac{1}{2}$
8 $(x + 3)^2 + 1$ **9** 25   **10** $x^2 + 3x + 5$

Trigonometry

2

Key points to remember

1 One radian is the angle subtended at the centre by an arc of length equal to the radius of the circle.

2 $360° = 2\pi^c$

3 The length s of an arc of a circle is given by $s = r\theta$, where r is the radius and θ is the angle in radians subtended by the arc at the centre of the circle.

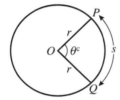

4 The area A of a sector of a circle is given by $A = \frac{1}{2}r^2\theta$, where r is the radius of the circle and θ is the angle in radians subtended by the arc at the centre of the circle.

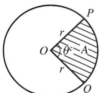

5 For the trigonometric ratios, sine, cosine and tangent:
- all are positive in the first quadrant
- only sine is positive in the second quadrant
- only tangent is positive in the third quadrant
- only cosine is positive in the fourth quadrant.

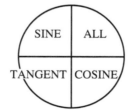

6 The trigonometric ratios of 30°, 45° and 60° angles are:

	30°	45°	60°
sin	$\dfrac{1}{2}$	$\dfrac{1}{\sqrt{2}}$	$\dfrac{\sqrt{3}}{2}$
cos	$\dfrac{\sqrt{3}}{2}$	$\dfrac{1}{\sqrt{2}}$	$\dfrac{1}{2}$
tan	$\dfrac{1}{\sqrt{3}}$	1	$\sqrt{3}$

7 The graph of $y = \sin x$:

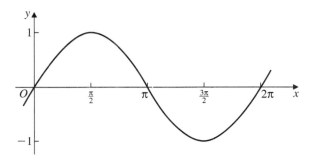

8 The graph of $y = \cos x$:

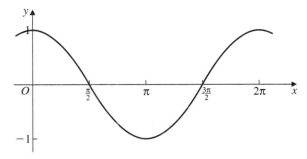

9 The graph of $y = \tan x$:

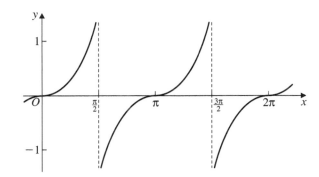

10 The graph of $y = \sin nx$, $y = \cos nx$ or $y = \tan nx$ ($n \in \mathbb{R}^+$) is the same shape as the graph of $y = \sin x$, $y = \cos x$ or $y = \tan x$, but n of each cycle of the curve fit into the range $0–2\pi^c$.

11 The graph of $y = n \sin x$, $y = n \cos x$ or $y = n \tan x$ ($n \in \mathbb{R}^+$) is the same shape as the graph of $y = \sin x$, $y = \cos x$ or $y = \tan x$, but with a stretch from the x-axis, scale factor n.

12 The graph of $y = \sin(x + n)$, $y = \cos(x + n)$ or $y = \tan(x + n)$ ($n \in \mathbb{R}^+$) is the same shape as the graph of $y = \sin x$, $y = \cos x$ or $y = \tan x$ but translated n radians to the left.

Similarly the graph of $y = \sin(x - n)$, $y = \cos(x - n)$ or $y = \tan(x - n)$ is translated n radians to the right.

13 $\tan \theta \equiv \dfrac{\sin \theta}{\cos \theta}$

14 $\sin^2 \theta + \cos^2 \theta \equiv 1$

Worked examination question 1

The diagram shows a circle, centre O and radius 5 cm. The sector OAB subtends an angle of 1.287^c at O.

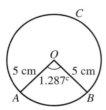

Calculate:

(a) the length of the major arc ACB
(b) the area of the major sector ACB.

Answer

(a) Reflex angle $AOB = 2\pi^c - 1.287^c$

$\qquad\qquad\qquad\quad \approx 4.996^c$

Using **2**

Length of arc $ACB \approx 5 \times 4.996$

$\qquad\qquad\quad = 24.98\,\text{cm}$ (2 d.p.)

Using **3**

(b) Area of sector $ACB \approx \frac{1}{2} \times 5^2 \times 4.996$

$\qquad\qquad\qquad = 62.45\,\text{cm}^2$ (2 d.p.)

Using **4**

Example 1

Sketch the graph of $y = \sin 2\theta$, $0 \leqslant \theta \leqslant 2\pi$.

Answer

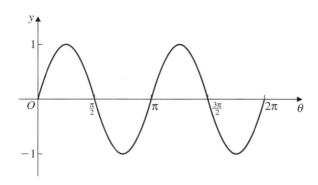

Using **7** and **10**

Example 2

Sketch the graph of $y = 3\cos\theta$, $0 \leqslant \theta \leqslant 2\pi$.

Answer

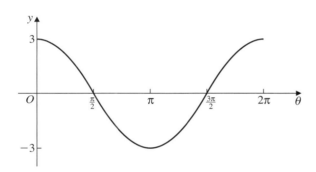

Using **7** and **11**

Example 3

Find the values of:
(a) $\sin 200°$
(b) $\cos 318°$
(c) $\tan 133°$
giving each answer to 3 decimal places.

Answer

(a) $\sin 200°$ lies in the third quadrant, so it is negative.

Using **5**

$$\begin{aligned}
\sin 200° &= -\sin(200° - 180°) \\
&= -\sin 20° \\
&= -0.342
\end{aligned}$$

(b) cos 318° lies in the fourth quadrant, so it is positive.

$$\cos 318° = +\cos(360° - 318°)$$
$$= \cos 42°$$
$$= 0.743$$

Using **5**

(c) tan 133° lies in the second quadrant, so it is negative.

$$\tan 133° = -\tan(180° - 133°)$$
$$= -\tan 47°$$
$$= -1.072$$

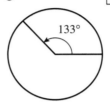

Using **5**

Example 4

(a) Express:
    (i) 30°   (ii) 108°
in radians in terms of π.

(b) Express:
    (i) 117°   (ii) 230°
in radians to 3 decimal places.

(c) Express:
    (i) 0.82^c (ii) 5^c
in degrees to 2 decimal places.

Answer

(a) (i) $360° = 2\pi$ radians

$$1° = \frac{2\pi}{360} \text{ radians}$$

$$30° = \frac{2\pi}{360} \times 30 \text{ radians}$$

$$= \frac{\pi}{6} \text{ radians}$$

Using **2**

    (ii) $360° = 2\pi$ radians

$$1° = \frac{2\pi}{360} \text{ radians}$$

$$108° = \frac{2\pi}{360} \times 108 \text{ radians}$$

$$= \frac{3\pi}{5} \text{ radians}$$

Using **2**

(b) (i) $360° = 2\pi$ radians

$$1° = \frac{2\pi}{360} \text{ radians}$$

$$117° = \frac{2\pi}{360} \times 117 \text{ radians}$$

$$= 2.042 \text{ radians (3 d.p.)}$$

Using **2**

(ii) $360° = 2\pi$ radians   Using ▨ 2

$1° = \dfrac{2\pi}{360}$ radians

$230° = \dfrac{2\pi}{360} \times 230$ radians

$= 4.014$ radians (3 d.p.)

(c) (i) $2\pi^c = 360$ degrees   Using ▨ 2

$1^c = \dfrac{360}{2\pi}$ degrees

$0.82^c = \dfrac{360}{2\pi} \times 0.82$ degrees

$= 46.98°$ (2 d.p.)

(ii) $2\pi^c = 360$ degrees   Using ▨ 2

$1^c = \dfrac{360}{2\pi}$ degrees

$5^c = \dfrac{360}{2\pi} \times 5$ degrees

$= 286.48°$ (2 d.p.)

Example 5

Find in surd form:
(a) $\sin 120°$
(b) $\cos 300°$
(c) $\tan 240°$

Answer

(a) $\sin 120°$ lies in the second quadrant and so is positive.   Using ▨ 5
So $\sin 120° = \sin(180° - 120°)$

$= \sin 60°$

$= \dfrac{\sqrt{3}}{2}$ Using ▨ 6

(b) $\cos 300°$ lies in the fourth quadrant and so is positive.   Using ▨ 5
So $\cos 300° = \cos(360° - 300°)$

$= \cos 60°$

$= \frac{1}{2}$ Using ▨ 6

(c) $\tan 240°$ lies in the third quadrant and so is positive.   Using ▨ 5
So $\tan 240° = \tan(240° - 180°)$

$= \tan 60°$
$= \sqrt{3}$ Using ▨ 6

Example 6

Find in surd form:
(a) $\tan 135°$
(b) $\tan 405°$

Answer

(a) $\tan 135°$ lies in the second quadrant and so is negative.

Using **5**

So $\tan 135° = -\tan(180° - 135°)$

$\qquad\qquad = -\tan 45°$

Using **6**

$\qquad\qquad = -1$

(b) $\tan 405°$ lies in the first quadrant and so is positive.

Using **5**

So $\tan 405° = \tan(405° - 360°)$

$\qquad\qquad = \tan 45°$

Using **6**

$\qquad\qquad = 1$

Worked examination question 2

Solve in the interval $0 \leqslant x \leqslant 360°$ the equations:
(a) $\sin x = -0.7$
(b) $\tan x = 1.488$
giving your answers to one decimal place.

Answer

(a) $\sin x = -0.7$

Since $\sin x$ is negative x must lie in the 3rd or 4th quadrant.

Using **5**

$\qquad \sin x = 0.7 \Rightarrow x = 44.42°$

So $\sin x = -0.7$

$\Rightarrow \qquad x = 180° + 44.42°$ **or** $x = 360° - 44.42°$

$\qquad\qquad x = 224.42° \qquad\qquad$ **or** $x = 315.58°$

$\qquad\qquad x = 224.4°$ (1 d.p.) **or** $x = 315.6°$ (1 d.p.)

(b) $\tan x = 1.488$

Since $\tan x$ is positive x must lie in the 1st or 3rd quadrants.

Using **5**

So $\tan x = 1.488$

$\Rightarrow \qquad x = 56.09°$ **or** $x = 180° + 56.09° = 236.09°$

$\qquad\qquad x = 56.1°$ (1 d.p.) **or** $x = 236.1°$ (1 d.p.)

Worked examination question 3

Find, to 2 decimal places, those values of x in the interval $0 \leqslant x \leqslant 2\pi$ for which:
(a) $\tan 2x = 4$
(b) $2 \tan x \sin x = 1$

Answer

(a) Since $\tan 2x$ is positive, $2x$ must lie in either the 1st or 3rd quadrants.

Using **5**

$$\tan 2x = 4$$
$$\Rightarrow \quad 2x = 1.326^c \text{ or } 2x = \pi^c + 1.326^c$$
or $\quad 2x = 2\pi^c + 1.326^c$ (1st quadrant again)
or $\quad 2x = 3\pi^c + 1.326^c$ (3rd quadrant again)

So $\quad x = 0.66^c, 2.23^c, 3.80^c, 5.38^c$

Using **10**

(b) $\qquad 2\tan x \sin x = 1$

$$\Rightarrow \quad \frac{2\sin x}{\cos x} \times \sin x = 1$$

Using **13**

$$\Rightarrow \quad 2\sin^2 x = \cos x$$
So $\qquad 2(1 - \cos^2 x) = \cos x$

Using **14**

$$\Rightarrow \quad 2\cos^2 x + \cos x - 2 = 0$$

$$\cos x = \frac{-1 \pm \sqrt{(1+16)}}{4}$$

Using the quadratic formula

$$= \frac{-1 \pm \sqrt{17}}{4}$$

$$= \frac{-1 \pm 4.123}{4}$$

$$= 0.7808 \text{ or } -1.2808$$

$$\cos x = 0.7808$$
$$\Rightarrow \quad x = 0.6749^c \text{ (1st quadrant)}$$

Using **5**

or $\quad x = 2\pi^c - 0.6749^c$ (4th quadrant)

Using **5**

So $\quad x = 0.68^c, 5.61^c$ (2 d.p.)

($\cos x = -1.2808$ produces no values of x since the minimum value of $\cos x$ is -1.)

Using **8**

Revision exercise 2

1 On the same axes, sketch the curves with equations:
$$y = 2\cos x$$
$$y = 3\cos(x - 30°)$$
for $-180° \leqslant x \leqslant 180°$.

2 On the same axes, sketch the graphs of:
$$y = \tan x$$
$$y = \tan x - 1$$
for $-\dfrac{\pi}{3} \leqslant x \leqslant \dfrac{\pi}{3}$.

3 On the same axes, sketch the curves with equations:

$$y = \sin x - 1$$
$$y = \sin x + 1$$
$$y = 2 \sin x$$

for $-1^c \leqslant x \leqslant 1^c$.

4 Copy the table and fill in the missing numbers, giving each number to 3 significant figures.

	θ	$\sin \theta$	$\cos \theta$	$\tan \theta$
(a)	$277°$		0.122	
(b)	$-35°$			-0.700
(c)	4.3^c	-0.916		
(d)	-0.52^c		0.868	
(e)	18^c			-1.14

5 Find the smallest positive value of x, to one decimal place, for which:

(a) $\sin x° = -0.892$

(b) $\tan x° = 7.81$

(c) $\sin 2x° = 0.35$

(d) $\cos^2 x° = 0.4$

(e) $\tan x° = -3$

6 Find, to 2 decimal places, the values of x for which $0 \leqslant x \leqslant 2\pi$ and:

(a) $\sin x^c = 0.57$

(b) $\cos x^c = -0.49$

(c) $\cos 2x^c = 0.24$

7 Find all the values of x in the interval $-180° \leqslant x \leqslant 720°$ for which:

(a) $\sin x = -\frac{1}{2}$

(b) $\tan x = \dfrac{1}{\sqrt{3}}$

8 Prove the identities:

(a) $\tan \theta + \dfrac{1}{\tan \theta} \equiv \dfrac{1}{\sin \theta \cos \theta}$

(b) $(1 - \sin t)^2 + (1 + \sin t)^2 \equiv 4 - 2 \cos^2 t$

(c) $\dfrac{\sin \theta}{\cos \theta + \sin \theta} - \dfrac{\cos \theta}{\cos \theta - \sin \theta} \equiv \dfrac{1}{2 \sin^2 \theta - 1}$

9 **(a)** Find the value of $\sin t$ and of $\cos t$, where $0 < t < 180°$ and $\tan t = -\frac{12}{5}$.

(b) The angle u is such that $270° < u < 360°$ and $\cos u = \frac{12}{37}$. Find the values of $\sin u$ and $\tan u$ as fractions in their lowest terms.

(c) The angle A is obtuse and $\sin A = \frac{8}{17}$. Find, as fractions, the values of $\cos A$ and $\tan A$.

10 Solve the equation $4 \sin^2 x - 7 \cos x - 2 = 0$ for the interval $0 \leqslant x \leqslant 2\pi$. Give your answers in radians to 2 decimal places.

11 Solve the equation $3 \sin^2 x - 2 \cos x - 2 = 0$ for the interval $0 \leqslant x \leqslant 2\pi$. Give your answers in radians to 2 decimal places.

12 **(a)** Find:
(i) the perimeter
(ii) the area
of the shaded sector.

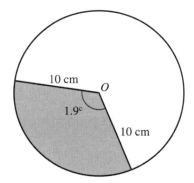

(b) The triangle ABC is equilateral and AB has length 12 cm. O is the centre of the circle through A, B and C. Find the area of the shaded region.

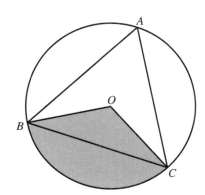

13 The areas of the two shaded
regions are equal.
Find:
(a) the value of θ
(b) the ratio of the perimeters
of the two shaded regions.

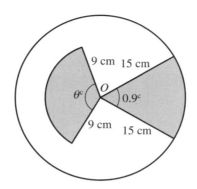

14 The square $ABCD$ has sides
of length 10 cm.
Circular arcs of radius 10 cm
are drawn from centres
A, B, C, D, as shown.
Find:
(a) the perimeter of the shaded
region
(b) the area of the shaded
region
giving your answers to
3 significant figures.

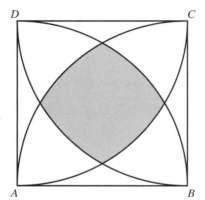

Test yourself	What to review

If your answer is incorrect:

1 Sketch the graphs of:
(a) $y = -\sin x$
(b) $y = \sin 3x$
for $0 \leqslant x \leqslant 360°$.

*Review Heinemann Book P1
pages 59–63*

2 Find, to 3 significant figures:
(a) $\sin 149°$
(b) $\cos 149°$
(c) $\tan 149°$

*Review Heinemann Book P1
pages 51–55*

3 Find the smallest positive value of x, to one decimal place,
for which $\cos x° = -0.12$.

*Review Heinemann Book P1
pages 71–74*

4 Find, to 2 decimal places, the value of x for which
$\tan\dfrac{x^c}{2} = 2.43$ and $0 \leqslant x \leqslant 2\pi$.

Review Heinemann Book P1 pages 71–74

---

5 Find all values of x in the interval $-180° \leqslant x \leqslant 720°$ for which $\cos x = \dfrac{1}{\sqrt{2}}$

Review Heinemann Book P1 pages 55–58

---

6 Prove the identity:
$(\cos y + \sin y)^2 \equiv 1 + 2\sin y \cos y$

Review Heinemann Book P1 pages 69–70

---

7 Find:
   (a) the length of the minor arc AB
   (b) the area of the shaded region.

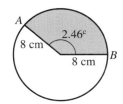

Review Heinemann Book P1 pages 48–51

Test yourself answers

1 (a)

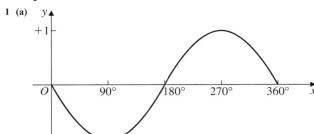

(b)

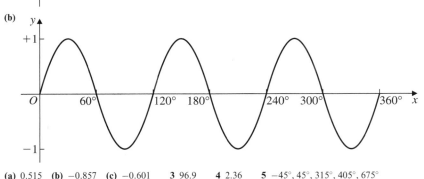

2 (a) 0.515 **(b)** -0.857 **(c)** -0.601 **3** 96.9   **4** 2.36   **5** $-45°, 45°, 315°, 405°, 675°$
6 $(\cos y + \sin y)^2 \equiv \cos^2 y + 2\cos y \sin y + \sin^2 y$
$\equiv (\cos^2 y + \sin^2 y) + 2\sin y \cos y$
$\equiv 1 + 2\sin y \cos y$
7 (a) 19.7 cm (3 s.f.) **(b)** 78.7 cm^2 (3 s.f.)

Coordinate geometry in the *xy*-plane

3

Key points to remember

1 The equation of a straight line with gradient m, passing through the point with coordinates (x_1, y_1) is
$$y - y_1 = m(x - x_1)$$

2 The equation of a straight line passing through the points with coordinates (x_1, y_1) and (x_2, y_2) is
$$\frac{y - y_1}{y_2 - y_1} = \frac{x - x_1}{x_2 - x_1}$$

3 The straight line with equation $ax + by + c = 0$ cuts the x-axis at the point $\left(\dfrac{-c}{a}, 0\right)$, cuts the y-axis at the point $\left(0, \dfrac{-c}{b}\right)$ and has gradient $\dfrac{-a}{b}$.

4 The lines with equations $y = m_1 x + c_1$ and $y = m_2 x + c_2$ are parallel if $m_1 = m_2$.

5 The lines with equations $y = m_1 x + c_1$ and $y = m_2 x + c_2$ are perpendicular if $m_1 m_2 = -1$.

6 The mid-point of the line segment joining (x_1, y_1) and (x_2, y_2) has coordinates $\left(\dfrac{x_1 + x_2}{2}, \dfrac{y_1 + y_2}{2}\right)$

Example 1

Find equations for the line segments:
(a) AB **(b)** BC
(c) OB **(d)** AC

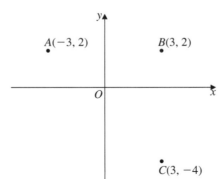

Answer

(a) *AB* is parallel to the *x*-axis and is at a distance 2 from that axis.
Its equation is $y = 2$.

(b) *BC* is parallel to the *y*-axis and is at a distance 3 from that axis.
Its equation is $x = 3$.

(c) *OB* has gradient $\frac{2}{3}$ and so has equation

$$y - 0 = \tfrac{2}{3}(x - 0)$$

Using **1**

i.e. $\qquad 3y = 2x$

(d) The line passing through *A* and *C* has equation

$$\frac{y - (-4)}{2 - (-4)} = \frac{x - 3}{-3 - 3}$$

Using **2**

So $\qquad \dfrac{y + 4}{2 + 4} = \dfrac{x - 3}{-6}$

$$\frac{y + 4}{6} = \frac{x - 3}{-6}$$

$$y + 4 = -x + 3$$

or $\qquad y + x + 1 = 0$

Example 2

Find an equation of the line perpendicular to the line joining
$A(-2, -4)$ and $B(4, -6)$ and which passes through *C*, the mid-point
of *AB*.

Answer

The gradient of $AB = \dfrac{-4 - (-6)}{-2 - 4}$

Using the fact that the gradient of a line joining (x_1, y_1) to (x_2, y_2) is $\dfrac{y_2 - y_1}{x_2 - x_1}$ (See Heinemann *Pure Mathematics 1* Chapter 3, page 79)

$$= \frac{-4 + 6}{-6}$$

$$= -\tfrac{1}{3}$$

So the gradient of the required line is *m* where
$-\frac{1}{3} \times m = -1$

Using **5**

i.e. $\quad m = 3$

The mid-point of *AB* is $\left(\dfrac{-2 + 4}{2}, \dfrac{-4 - 6}{2} \right)$

Using **6**

$$= (1, -5)$$

So an equation of the required line is:

$$y - (-5) = 3(x - 1)$$

Using **1**

$$y + 5 = 3x - 3$$

$$y - 3x + 8 = 0$$

Example 3

Find an equation of the line parallel to the line with equation $y = -2x + 5$ and which passes through the point with coordinates $(5, -6)$.

Answer

The gradient of $y = -2x + 5$ is -2.

> Since the gradient of $y = mx + c$ is m.

So the gradient of the parallel line is also -2.
An equation of the required line is:

> Using **4**

$$y - (-6) = -2(x - 5)$$
$$y + 6 = -2x + 10$$
$$y + 2x = 4$$

> Using **1**

Worked examination question 1

The line with equation $12x - 9y = 40$ meets the *x*-axis at A and the *y*-axis at B. The quadrilateral $AOBC$ is a rectangle, where O is the origin.
Find:
(a) the length of AB
(b) the coordinates of C
(c) the area of $AOBC$.

Answer

A diagram of the situation is shown:
(a) The line cuts the *x*-axis where
$y = 0$
i.e. where $12x = 40$

$$\Rightarrow \qquad x = \frac{10}{3}$$

The line cuts the *y*-axis where $x = 0$
i.e. where $-9y = 40$

$$\Rightarrow \qquad y = \frac{-40}{9}$$

So A is $\left(\dfrac{10}{3}, 0\right)$ and B is $\left(0, \dfrac{-40}{9}\right)$

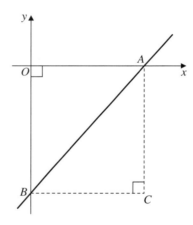

The length of AB is:

$$\sqrt{\left[\left(\frac{10}{3} - 0\right)^2 + \left(0 + \frac{40}{9}\right)^2\right]}$$

> Since the length of the line joining (x_1, y_1) to (x_2, y_2) is $\sqrt{[(x_1 - x_2)^2 + (y_1 - y_2)^2]}$

$$= \sqrt{\left[\frac{100}{9} + \frac{1600}{81}\right]} = \sqrt{\left[\frac{900 + 1600}{81}\right]}$$

$$= \sqrt{\frac{2500}{81}} = \frac{50}{9} \text{ units}$$

(b) From the diagram it is clear that C is the point $\left(\dfrac{10}{3}, \dfrac{-40}{9}\right)$.

(c) The area of rectangle $AOBC$ is

$$\tfrac{10}{3} \times \tfrac{40}{9} = \tfrac{400}{27} = 14\tfrac{22}{27} \text{ units}^2$$

Revision exercise 3

1 Find an equation of the straight line that:
   (a) has gradient $-\frac{2}{5}$ and meets the *x*-axis at $(-4, 0)$
   (b) passes through $(\frac{1}{2}, \frac{1}{3})$ and $(-\frac{1}{4}, \frac{2}{3})$
   (c) has gradient 4 and meets the *y*-axis at $(0, -5)$
   (d) has gradient 1 and passes through the point of
   intersection of the lines with equations $y + x = 1$ and
   $y + 4x + 8 = 0$.

2 The lines *l* and *m* have equations $5x - y = 7$ and $3y - 2x = 5$
   respectively. They meet at the point *A*.
   The points *B* and *C* have coordinates $(1, -2)$ and $(-1, 1)$
   respectively.
   (a) Show that *B* lies on *l* and *C* lies on *m*.
   (b) Find the coordinates of *A*.
   (c) Prove that $\angle ACB = 90°$.

3 (a) Find, in the form $y = mx + c$, an equation of the line
   joining $P(0, 3)$ and $Q(3, 9)$.
   The line *PQ* meets the line with equation $x + 2y = 11$ at *R*.
   (b) Find the coordinates of *R*.
   (c) Given that *S* is the point $(13, 0)$, calculate the length
   of *RS*.

4 (a) Prove that the points $A(9, 11)$, $B(-5, 3)$, and $C(3, -1)$ are
   the vertices of a right-angled triangle.
   Find:
   (b) the area of $\triangle ABC$
   (c) the coordinates of *D* if *ACBD* is a rectangle.

5 Find an equation of the straight line that:
   (a) passes through the origin *O* and is parallel to the line
   joining the points $(2, 6)$ and $(-1, 5)$.
   (b) passes through *O* and is perpendicular to the line joining
   the points $(3, -5)$ and $(5, -3)$.
   (c) passes through the mid-point of the line joining $A(5, -3)$
   to $B(3, -1)$ and is also perpendicular to this line (often called
   the **perpendicular bisector** of *AB*).

6 The point (p, q) is equidistant from the points $A(1, 2)$, $B(-1, -1)$ and $C(2, -2)$.
Show that $p = \frac{21}{22}$ and find the value of q.

7 Find an equation of the perpendicular bisector of the straight line joining the points with coordinates $(-2, 7)$ and $(8, 1)$.
Prove that the point $(12, 19)$ lies on this perpendicular bisector.

8 The curve with equation $x^2 + 4y^2 - 4x = 9$ meets the line $3x - 2y = 9$ in the points P and Q.
(a) Find the coordinates of P and Q.
(b) The line l is perpendicular to PQ and passes through M, the mid-point of PQ.
Find an equation of l.

9 The lines with equations $3x - 4y = 1$ and $4x - 3y = \frac{1}{6}$ meet at the point A.
(a) Find an equation of the line OA, where O is the origin.
The line through A which is perpendicular to OA meets the x-axis at P and the y-axis at Q.
(b) Find the length of PQ, giving your answer to 3 decimal places.

Test yourself	What to review
	If your answer is incorrect:
1 Find an equation of the straight line that has gradient $\frac{2}{3}$ and passes through the point $(-3, 5)$.	*Review Heinemann Book P1 pages 77–79*
2 Find an equation of the straight line that passes through the points $(-2, 5)$ and $(3, 10)$.	*Review Heinemann Book P1 pages 79–82*
3 Find an equation of the straight line that passes through $(3, -2)$ and is parallel to the line with equation $4x - 7y = 11$.	*Review Heinemann Book P1 pages 85–88*
4 Find an equation of the straight line that passes through $(3, -2)$ and is perpendicular to the line with equation $4x - 7y = 11$.	*Review Heinemann Book P1 pages 85–88*

5 The line *l* passes through the points $A(5, 6)$ and $B(-5, 10)$.
   (a) Find an equation of *l*.
   The line *l* meets the *x*-axis at *P* and the line with equation
   $y = x + 22$ at *Q*.
   (b) Find the distance between *P* and *Q*.

Review Heinemann Book P1
pages 79–85

6 Find the coordinates of the mid-point of *AB* where *A* has
   coordinates $(-5, 7)$ and *B* has coordinates $(3, -9)$.

Review Heinemann Book P1
pages 88–91

Test yourself answers

1 $3y - 2x = 21$ **2** $y = x + 7$ **3** $7y - 4x + 26 = 0$ **4** $4y + 7x - 13 = 0$ **5 (a)** $5y + 2x = 40$ **(b)** $6\sqrt{29}$ units   **6** $(-1, -1)$

Sequences and series

4

Key points to remember

1. A sequence is a succession of numbers formed by following a rule.

2. The numbers in a sequence are called **terms** and the nth term is called the general term.

3. A sequence whose nth term approaches a finite number as n approaches infinity is called a **convergent sequence**.
   A sequence whose nth term approaches infinity as n approaches infinity is called a **divergent sequence**.
   A sequence whose successive terms vary between a and b $(a, b \in \mathbb{Q})$ is called an **oscillating sequence**.

4. If $u_1, u_2, u_3, \ldots, u_n$ is a finite sequence then $u_1 + u_2 + u_3 + \ldots + u_n$ is called a **finite series**, sometimes written $\sum\limits_{r=1}^{n} u_r$.
   Similarly, if $u_1, u_2, u_3, \ldots, u_n, \ldots$ is an infinite sequence then $u_1 + u_2 + u_3 + \ldots + u_n + \ldots$ is called an **infinite series**, sometimes written $\sum\limits_{r=1}^{\infty} u_r$

5. In an arithmetic series each term is obtained by adding a constant quantity (called the **common difference**) to the previous term.

6. An arithmetic series with first term a and common difference d, has nth term $a + (n-1)d$.

7. The sum of the arithmetic series with n terms
   $$a + (a+d) + (a+2d) + \ldots + (L-d) + L,$$
   where L is the last term, is
   $$\frac{n}{2}(a+L)$$

8. The sum of the arithmetic series with n terms
   $$a + (a+d) + (a+2d) + \ldots + [a + (n-1)d]$$
   is $\quad \dfrac{n}{2}[2a + (n-1)d]$

9 The sum of the first n natural numbers is

$$\tfrac{1}{2}n(n+1)$$

10 A series where each term is obtained by multiplying the previous term by a fixed number r (called the common ratio), where r can take any value except 0, 1 or -1, is called a **geometric series**.

11 The nth term of the geometric series $a + ar + ar^2 + \ldots$ is ar^{n-1}.

12 The sum of the finite geometric series with n terms $a + ar + ar^2 + \ldots + ar^{n-1}$ is

$$\frac{a(1-r^n)}{1-r} = \frac{a(r^n-1)}{r-1}$$

13 The sum of the infinite geometric series

$$a + ar + ar^2 + \ldots + ar^{n-1} + \ldots$$

is

$$\frac{a}{1-r} \text{ provided } |r| < |$$

Example 1

A sequence of terms has nth term u_n, where $u_n = 3 - 4n^2$.
Find the first 4 terms of the sequence.

Answer

$u_1 = 3 - 4(1^2) = 3 - 4 = -1$

$u_2 = 3 - 4(2^2) = 3 - 16 = -13$

$u_3 = 3 - 4(3^2) = 3 - 36 = -33$

$u_4 = 3 - 4(4^2) = 3 - 64 = -61$

Using **1** and **2**

Example 2

Find the sum of the first 85 terms of the arithmetic series with first term -17 and common difference 1.5.

Answer

If $a = -17$ and $d = 1.5$ and the arithmetic series of 85 terms is $a + (a+d) + (a+2d) + \ldots + (a+84d)$ then its sum is

$$S_{85} = \tfrac{85}{2}[2 \times (-17) + (84 \times 1.5)]$$

Using **8**

$$= 42.5[-34 + 126]$$

$$= 42.5 \times 92$$

$$= 3910$$

Example 3

The sum to n terms of an arithmetic series is $3n^2 + 6n$.
Find:

(a) u_n

(b) $\displaystyle\sum_{n=8}^{17} u_n$

where u_n is the nth term.

Answer

(a) $S_n = 3n^2 + 6n$

But the sum to n terms of an arithmetic series is

$$S_n = u_1 + u_2 + u_3 + \ldots + u_n$$

and $S_{n-1} = u_1 + u_2 + u_3 + \ldots + u_{n-1}$

$\boxed{\text{Using } \boxed{4}}$

So $u_n = S_n - S_{n-1}$

$$= 3n^2 + 6n - \left[3(n-1)^2 + 6(n-1)\right]$$
$$= 3n^2 + 6n - \left[3n^2 - 6n + 3 + 6n - 6\right]$$
$$= 3n^2 + 6n - 3n^2 + 6n - 3 - 6n + 6$$
$$= 6n + 3$$

(b) $\displaystyle\sum_{n=8}^{17} u_n = u_8 + u_9 + \ldots + u_{17}$

$$= u_1 + u_2 + \ldots + u_{17} - (u_1 + u_2 + \ldots + u_7)$$
$$= S_{17} - S_7$$
$$= 3(17^2) + (6 \times 17) - \left[3(7^2) + (6 \times 7)\right]$$
$$= (3 \times 289) + 102 - \left[(3 \times 49) + 42\right]$$
$$= 867 + 102 - 147 - 42$$
$$= 780$$

Example 4

A geometric series has first term 1000 and common ratio 0.75.
Find:

(a) the 20th term of the series

(b) the sum of the first 25 terms of the series

(c) the sum to infinity of the series.

Answer

(a) $a = 1000$ and $r = 0.75$

$$u_{20} = 1000 \times 0.75^{20-1} = 1000 \times 0.75^{19}$$

$\boxed{\text{Using } \boxed{11}}$

$$= 4.228 \text{ (4 s.f.)}$$

(b) $S_{25} = \dfrac{a(1 - r^{25})}{1 - r}$

$\boxed{\text{Using } \boxed{12}}$

$$= \frac{1000(1 - 0.75^{25})}{1 - 0.75}$$
$$= \frac{1000(1 - 0.75^{25})}{0.25}$$
$$= 4000(1 - 0.75^{25})$$
$$= 3997 \text{ (4 s.f.)}$$

(c) Since $|0.75| < 1$ the series has a sum to infinity given by

$$\frac{1000}{1 - 0.75}$$

Using **13**

$$= \frac{1000}{0.25}$$

$$= 4000$$

Worked examination question 1 [E]

The sum of the first and third terms of a geometric series is $6\frac{2}{3}$.
The sum of the second and fourth terms is $2\frac{2}{9}$.
Find the first term and the common ratio of the series.

Answer

$$a + ar^2 = 6\tfrac{2}{3} \quad \text{①}$$

Using **11**

$$ar + ar^3 = 2\tfrac{2}{9} \quad \text{②}$$

$$a(1 + r^2) = 6\tfrac{2}{3} \quad \text{①}$$

$$ar(1 + r^2) = 2\tfrac{2}{9} \quad \text{②}$$

②÷① gives $\dfrac{ar(1 + r^2)}{a(1 + r^2)} = \dfrac{\frac{20}{9}}{\frac{20}{3}}$

$$r = \tfrac{20}{9} \times \tfrac{3}{20} = \tfrac{1}{3}$$

From ① $a(1 + \tfrac{1}{9}) = \tfrac{20}{3}$

$$a = \tfrac{20}{3} \times \tfrac{9}{10} = 6$$

Worked examination question 2 [E]

The rth term of a series is u_r, where $u_r = 2r - 1$.

Calculate $\displaystyle\sum_{r=1}^{21} u_r$

Answer

$$\sum_{r=1}^{21} u_r = u_1 + u_2 + u_3 + \ldots + u_{21}$$

$$= [(2 \times 1) - 1] + [(2 \times 2) - 1] + [(2 \times 3) - 1] + \ldots + [(2 \times 21) - 1]$$

$$= 1 + 3 + 5 + \ldots + 41$$

This is an arithmetic series with first term 1 and last term 41.

So $S_{21} = \tfrac{21}{2}[1 + 41]$

Using **7**

$$= \tfrac{21}{2} \times 42$$

$$= 21 \times 21$$

$$= 441$$

Worked examination question 3 [E]

The numbers $(t + 3)$, $(5t - 3)$ and $(7t + 3)$ are 3 consecutive terms of a geometric series of positive terms.
(a) Calculate the value of t.
(b) With this value of t and given that $(t + 3)$, $(5t - 3)$ and $(7t + 3)$ are the second, third and fourth terms respectively of the series, calculate the sum of the first 10 terms of the series.

Answer

(a) If $\quad t + 3 = ar^n$

then $5t - 3 = ar^{n+1}$

and $\ 7t + 3 = ar^{n+2}$

Using **11**

So $\qquad \dfrac{5t - 3}{t + 3} = \dfrac{ar^{n+1}}{ar^n} = r$

and also $\dfrac{7t + 3}{5t - 3} = \dfrac{ar^{n+2}}{ar^{n+1}} = r$

Thus $\quad \dfrac{7t + 3}{5t - 3} = \dfrac{5t - 3}{t + 3}$

Using $(a - b)^2 \equiv a^2 - 2ab + b^2$

$(7t + 3)(t + 3) = (5t - 3)^2$

$7t^2 + 24t + 9 = 25t^2 - 30t + 9$

$0 = 18t^2 - 54t$

$0 = 18t(t - 3)$

So $t = 0$ or 3.
But if $t = 0$, then $5t - 3 = -3$.
This cannot be, since the geometric series consists only of positive terms.
So $t = 3$.

(b) Using $t = 3$ and $u_2 = t + 3$, $u_3 = 5t - 3$, $u_4 = 7t + 3$

$u_2 = ar = 3 + 3 = 6$

$u_3 = ar^2 = (5 \times 3) - 3 = 12$

Using **11**

$u_4 = ar^3 = (7 \times 3) + 3 = 24$

$\dfrac{u_3}{u_2} = \dfrac{12}{6} = \dfrac{ar^2}{ar} = r$

So $\qquad r = 2$

$u_2 = ar = 2a = 6$

So $\qquad a = 3$

$S_{10} = \displaystyle\sum_{n=1}^{10} 3 \times 2^{n-1}$

$= \dfrac{3(2^{10} - 1)}{2 - 1} = \dfrac{3(1024 - 1)}{1}$

Using **12**

$= 3 \times 1023 = 3069$

Revision exercise 4

1 The first two terms of an arithmetic series are u_1 and u_2. The
   nth term is u_n and the sum to n terms is S_n.
   Copy and complete the table:

	u_1	u_2	n	u_n	S_n
(a)	8.5	6.9	50		
(b)	8		16		488
(c)	7	10		130	
(d)		8		84	1800

2 The first two terms of a geometric series are v_1 and v_2. The
   nth term is v_n and the sum to n terms is S_n. Copy and
   complete the table, giving answers to 3 s.f. where necessary.

	v_1	v_2	n	v_n	S_n
(a)	100	80	15		
(b)	0.4	−0.6	10		
(c)	−0.125	0.25		−32	
(d)	125	75			297.92

3 The first term of an arithmetic series is -12 and the last term
   is 22. The sum of all the terms of the series is 260.
   Find the common difference of the series.

4 For the geometric series:
   $$v_1 + v_2 + v_3 + \ldots + v_n$$
   it is known that:
   $$v_3 - v_2 = 5 \text{ and } v_4 - v_3 = 6$$
   Prove that the common ratio is $\frac{6}{5}$ and find the first term.
   Hence find the sum of the first 4 terms of the series.

5 An arithmetic series has the following properties:
   (i) the sum of the fourth and ninth terms is 58
   (ii) the sum of the first 26 terms is 390.
   (a) Find the first term and the common difference.
   (b) Find the smallest integer value of n for which the sum to
   n terms of the series is negative.

6 The numbers m, n and mn are the first 3 terms of a geometric series.
The numbers m, n and $m + n$ are the first 3 terms of an arithmetic series.
Find the value of m and the value of n, both of which are non-zero.

7 Find the sum of all the integers between 100 and 1000 which are divisible by 11 exactly.

8 The seventh term of a geometric series is -20 and the tenth term is 2.5.
Find the sum to infinity of this series.

9 The sum of the first three terms of a geometric series is $\frac{65}{9}$ and the sum to infinity is $7\frac{1}{2}$.
(a) Find the first term and the common ratio.
(b) Find the least number of terms required so that their sum differs from $7\frac{1}{2}$ by less than 10^{-4}.

10 (a) A geometric series has first term $\sqrt{6}$ and second term $2\sqrt{3}$.
Find the common ratio and the fifth term of the series.
(b) Find the value of $\displaystyle\sum_{n=3}^{17}(2n - 5)$.
(c) The sum to n terms of an arithmetic series with first term -38 and common difference 2 is 550.
Find the value of n.

Test yourself	**What to review**
	If your answer is incorrect:
1 The first term of an arithmetic series is 7 and the second term is 12. Find the 22nd term and the sum of the first 22 terms of the series.	*Review Heinemann Book P1 pages 112–116*
2 The first term of a geometric series is 7 and the second term is 14. Find the 12th term of the series and the sum of the first 12 terms.	*Review Heinemann Book P1 pages 119–124*

3 Find the positive constants a and b such that
　　 0.25, a, 9
are consecutive terms of a geometric series and
　　 0.25, a, $9 - b$
are consecutive terms of an arithmetic series.

Review Heinemann Book P1
pages 112–114 and 119–120

4 The first and third terms of an arithmetic series are a and b respectively. The sum of the first n terms of the series is S_n. Find S_4 in terms of a and b.

Review Heinemann Book P1
pages 112–119

5 A geometric series with first term 3 converges to the sum 2. Find the fifth term in the series.

Review Heinemann Book P1
pages 121–124

Test yourself answers

1 112, 1309　　**2** 14 336, 28 665　　**3** $a = 1\frac{1}{2}, b = 6\frac{1}{4}$　　**4** $a + 3b$　　**5** $\frac{3}{16}$

Differentiation

5

Key points to remember

1 The gradient of a curve with equation $y = f(x)$ at the point $x = a$, $y = b$ is the gradient of the tangent to the curve at the point (a, b).

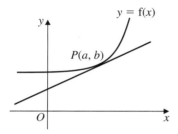

2 The rate of change of y with respect to x is given by $\dfrac{\mathrm{d}y}{\mathrm{d}x}$.

This is called the **derivative** or **differential coefficient** of y with respect to x.

3 If $y = f(x)$, then $\dfrac{\mathrm{d}y}{\mathrm{d}x} = f'(x)$.

f' is often called the **derived function** of f.

4 If $y = x^n$, then

$$\frac{\mathrm{d}y}{\mathrm{d}x} = nx^{n-1}$$

5 If $y = kx^n$, where k is a constant, then

$$\frac{\mathrm{d}y}{\mathrm{d}x} = knx^{n-1}$$

6 If $y = u \pm v$, where u and v are functions of x, then

$$\frac{\mathrm{d}y}{\mathrm{d}x} = \frac{\mathrm{d}u}{\mathrm{d}x} \pm \frac{\mathrm{d}v}{\mathrm{d}x}$$

7 A function which increases in the interval from $x = a$ to $x = b$ is called an **increasing function** in the interval (a, b).
A function that decreases in the interval from $x = a$ to $x = b$ is called a **decreasing function** in the interval (a, b).

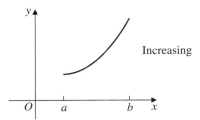
Increasing

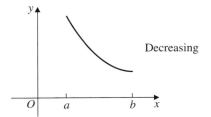
Decreasing

8 If $y = f(x)$, then $\dfrac{d^2y}{dx^2} = f''(x)$ is called the **second derivative** of y with respect to x.

$$\frac{d^2y}{dx^2} = \frac{d}{dx}\left(\frac{dy}{dx}\right) = \frac{d}{dx}[f'(x)] = f''(x)$$

9 If $y = f(x)$, then $\dfrac{d^n y}{dx^n} = f^{(n)}(x)$ is called the **nth derivative** of y with respect to x.

10 A point on the curve with equation $y = f(x)$ for which $f'(x) = 0$ is called a **turning** (or stationary) **point** of the curve.

11 If $f'(x) = 0$ and $f''(x) < 0$, the turning point is a **maximum**.

12 If $f'(x) = 0$ and $f''(x) > 0$, the turning point is a **minimum**.

13 If $f'(x) = 0$, $f''(x) = 0$ and $f'''(x) \neq 0$, the turning point is a **point of inflexion**.

14 An equation of the tangent at $P(a, b)$ to the curve with equation $y = f(x)$ is
$$y - b = f'(a)(x - a)$$

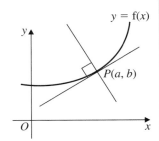

15 An equation of the normal at $P(a, b)$ to the curve with equation $y = f(x)$ is

$$y - b = -\frac{1}{f'(a)}(x - a)$$

Example 1

Differentiate with respect to x:

(a) $y = x^4$ (b) $y = 6x^3$

(c) $y = \sqrt{x^3}$ (d) $y = \dfrac{5}{x^2}$

Answer

(a) $y = x^4$

$\Rightarrow \quad \dfrac{dy}{dx} = 4x^3$ | Using **4** |

(b) $y = 6x^3$

$\Rightarrow \quad \dfrac{dy}{dx} = 18x^2$ | Using **5** |

(c) $y = \sqrt{x^3}$

So $y = x^{\frac{3}{2}}$ | Since $\sqrt{x^a} = (x^a)^{\frac{1}{2}} = x^{\frac{a}{2}}$ |

$\Rightarrow \quad \dfrac{dy}{dx} = \frac{3}{2}x^{\frac{3}{2}-1} = \frac{3}{2}x^{\frac{1}{2}} = \frac{3}{2}\sqrt{x}$ | Using **4** |

(d) $y = \dfrac{5}{x^2}$

So $y = 5x^{-2}$ | Since $\dfrac{1}{x^n} = x^{-n}$ |

$\Rightarrow \quad \dfrac{dy}{dx} = 5(-2x^{-2-1})$ | Using **5** |

$\qquad\qquad = -10x^{-3} = \dfrac{-10}{x^3}$

Example 2

Given that $y = (x^2 - 3)^2$, find the rate of change of y with respect to x at $x = \frac{1}{2}$.

Answer

$\qquad y = (x^2 - 3)^2$

$\qquad\quad = (x^2)^2 + 2(-3x^2) + (-3)^2$ | Using $(a - b)^2 \equiv a^2 - 2ab + b^2$ |

$\qquad y = x^4 - 6x^2 + 9$

$\Rightarrow \quad \dfrac{dy}{dx} = 4x^3 - 12x + 0$ | Using **4**, **5** and **6** and remembering that if $y = k$, where k is a constant, then $y = kx^0$ and so $\dfrac{dy}{dx} = k \times 0 \times x^{-1} = 0$ |

$\qquad\qquad = 4x^3 - 12x$

At $x = \frac{1}{2}$, $\dfrac{dy}{dx} = 4(\frac{1}{2})^3 - 12(\frac{1}{2})$

$\qquad\qquad\quad = (4 \times \frac{1}{8}) - 6$

$\qquad\qquad\quad = \frac{1}{2} - 6 = -5\frac{1}{2}$

The rate of change of y with respect to x is $-5\frac{1}{2}$ at $x = \frac{1}{2}$. | Using **2** |

Example 3
Find the second derivative of x^4.

Answer

Let $\quad y = x^4$

then $\quad \dfrac{dy}{dx} = 4x^3$

Using **4**

So $\quad \dfrac{d^2y}{dx^2} = 4 \times 3 \times x^{3-1}$

Using **5** and **8**

$\qquad\qquad = 12x^2$

Worked examination question 1

A toy which costs £C to manufacture takes t hours to make, where

$$C = \frac{9}{8t^3} + \frac{2t^2}{9}.$$

(a) Find the value of t for which C is least.
(b) Find the least value of C and prove that it is a minimum.

Answer

(a) If $\quad C = \dfrac{9}{8t^3} + \dfrac{2t^2}{9}$

then $\quad C = \frac{9}{8}t^{-3} + \frac{2}{9}t^2$

Using $\dfrac{1}{x^a} = x^{-a}$

So $\quad \dfrac{dC}{dt} = \frac{9}{8}(-3)t^{-4} + \frac{2}{9}(2)t$

Using **5** and **6**

$\qquad\qquad = -\frac{27}{8}t^{-4} + \frac{4}{9}t$

Turning points occur where $\dfrac{dC}{dt} = 0$

i.e. where

$$-\tfrac{27}{8}t^{-4} + \tfrac{4}{9}t = 0$$

Using **10**

$$\Rightarrow \quad -\frac{27}{8t^4} + \frac{4t}{9} = 0$$

Using $t^{-4} = \dfrac{1}{t^4}$

$$(-27 \times 9) + (4t \times 8t^4) = 0$$

$$-243 + 32t^5 = 0$$

$$32t^5 = 243$$

$$t^5 = \tfrac{243}{32}$$

$$t = \tfrac{3}{2}$$

(b) $\qquad \dfrac{dC}{dt} = -\frac{27}{8}t^{-4} + \frac{4}{9}t$

$$\Rightarrow \quad \frac{d^2C}{dt^2} = -\frac{27}{8}(-4)t^{-5} + \frac{4}{9}$$

Using **5**, **6** and **8**

$$= \frac{27}{2}t^{-5} + \frac{4}{9}$$

At $t = \frac{3}{2}$, $\dfrac{d^2 C}{dt^2} = \frac{27}{2} \times \left(\frac{3}{2}\right)^{-5} + \frac{4}{9}$

$\qquad\qquad\qquad = \frac{27}{2} \times \left(\frac{2}{3}\right)^5 + \frac{4}{9}$

$\qquad\qquad\qquad = \frac{27}{2} \times \frac{32}{243} + \frac{4}{9}$

$\qquad\qquad\qquad = \frac{16}{9} + \frac{4}{9} = \frac{20}{9} > 0$

So at $t = \frac{3}{2}$, C is a minimum.

$\boxed{\text{Using } \blacksquare 12}$

The minimum value of C is given by

$$\frac{9}{8}\left(\frac{3}{2}\right)^{-3} + \frac{2}{9}\left(\frac{3}{2}\right)^2$$

$$= \frac{9}{8}\left(\frac{2}{3}\right)^3 + \frac{2}{9}\left(\frac{3}{2}\right)^2$$

$$= \left(\frac{9}{8} \times \frac{8}{27}\right) + \left(\frac{2}{9} \times \frac{9}{4}\right)$$

$$= \frac{1}{3} + \frac{1}{2} = \frac{5}{6}$$

So the least value of C is $\frac{5}{6}$.

Worked examination question 2

Find an equation of the tangent and an equation of the normal to the curve with equation $y = x^{\frac{4}{3}}$ at the point on the curve where $x = 8$.

Answer

$$y = x^{\frac{4}{3}}$$

$\Rightarrow \qquad\qquad \dfrac{dy}{dx} = \frac{4}{3} x^{\frac{1}{3}}$

$\boxed{\text{Using } \blacksquare 5}$

At $x = 8$, $\dfrac{dy}{dx} = \frac{4}{3} \times 8^{\frac{1}{3}}$

$\qquad\qquad\qquad = \frac{4}{3} \times 2$

$\qquad\qquad\qquad = \frac{8}{3}$

At $x = 8$, $y = 8^{\frac{4}{3}} = (2^3)^{\frac{4}{3}} = 2^4 = 16$

An equation of the tangent at $(8, 16)$ is

$\qquad y - 16 = \frac{8}{3}(x - 8)$

$\boxed{\text{Using } \blacksquare 14}$

An equation of the normal at $(8, 16)$ is

$\qquad y - 16 = -\frac{3}{8}(x - 8)$

$\boxed{\text{Using } \blacksquare 15}$

Example 4

Find the maximum rectangular area that can be fenced off from a rectangular field by 100 m of fencing using
(a) one of the existing walls of the field,
(b) two of the existing walls of the field, which are at right angles to each other.

Answer

(a) Let y metres be the length of the rectangle and x metres be the width.

The area, $A\,\mathrm{m}^2$, is given by $A = xy$

The total length of fencing is

$$100 = 2x + y$$

So $\quad y = 100 - 2x$

Therefore $A = x(100 - 2x)$

$$A = 100x - 2x^2$$

$$\frac{\mathrm{d}A}{\mathrm{d}x} = 100 - 4x$$

Turning points occur where $\dfrac{\mathrm{d}A}{\mathrm{d}x} = 0$

i.e. where $100 - 4x = 0$

$$4x = 100$$

$$x = 25$$

$$\frac{\mathrm{d}^2A}{\mathrm{d}x^2} = 0 - 4 = -4 < 0$$

So $x = 25$ produces a maximum value of A.

Thus the maximum value of A is given by

$$A = 25(100 - 50)$$

$$= 25 \times 50 = 1250$$

So the maximum area is $1250\,\mathrm{m}^2$.

(b) Let y metres be the length of the rectangle and x metres be the width.

Area $A = xy$

The total length of fencing is

$$100 = x + y$$

so $\quad y = 100 - x$

Thus $\quad A = x(100 - x)$

$$A = 100x - x^2$$

$$\frac{\mathrm{d}A}{\mathrm{d}x} = 100 - 2x$$

Turning points occur where $\dfrac{\mathrm{d}A}{\mathrm{d}x} = 0$

i.e. where $100 - 2x = 0$

$$\Rightarrow \qquad 2x = 100$$

$$x = 50$$

$$\frac{\mathrm{d}^2A}{\mathrm{d}x^2} = 0 - 2 = -2 < 0$$

So $x = 50$ produces a maximum value of A.

Thus the maximum value of A is given by

$$A = 50(100 - 50)$$

$$= 50 \times 50 = 2500$$

So the maximum area is $2500\,\mathrm{m}^2$.

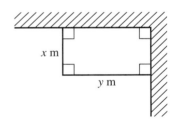

Revision exercise 5

1 Find the derivative of:

   (a) $x^3 - 4x$ (b) $3x^5 - 5x^3$ (c) $2x^2 - \dfrac{3}{x}$

2 Find the differential coefficient of:

   (a) $2x^{\frac{1}{2}} - 3x^{\frac{2}{3}}$ (b) $(x^{\frac{1}{2}} - x^{-\frac{1}{2}})^3$ (c) $(x^2 - 1)(x^{-2} + 1)$

3 Find an equation of the tangent and of the normal at the points $(2, 1)$ and $(1, -1)$ on the curve with equation $y = x^2 - x - 1$.

4 Prove that the tangent at $(-2, -12)$ to the curve with equation $y = x^3 - x^2$ is parallel to the line $y = 16x - 7$.
   Find also the equation of the normal at $(2, 4)$ to the curve with equation $y = x^3 - x^2$, giving your answer in the form $y = mx + c$.

5 For the function f in each case, find the set of values of x for which:

   (i) f is increasing   (ii) f is decreasing

   (a) $f(x) \equiv x^3 - 75x$ (b) $f(x) \equiv -2x + \dfrac{1}{x^2}$

   (c) $f(x) \equiv 1 + 2x^2 - \frac{1}{4}x^4$

6 Find and distinguish the nature of each turning point on the curves with equations $y = f(x)$ where:

   (a) $f(x) \equiv x^3 - 27x$ (b) $f(x) \equiv (1 - 2x)x^2$

   (c) $f(x) \equiv \frac{1}{3}x^{-3} + \frac{1}{16}x$

7 A right circular cylinder is made so that the sum of its radius and its height is $2\,\text{m}$. Given that the radius of the cylinder is r metres and that its volume is $V\,\text{m}^3$, prove that:
   $$V = 2\pi r^2 - \pi r^3.$$
   Given further that r can vary, find the volume of the largest cylinder that can be made.
   Prove that this volume is the maximum.

8 (a) Given that $f(x) = (x^2 + 3)(x - 2)$, find the value of $f''(2)$ and $f''(-1)$.

   (b) The curve with equation $y = \dfrac{a}{x} - bx^2$ passes through the point $P(2, -2)$. The gradient of the tangent to the curve at P is -4.
   Find the value of the constants a and b.

9 Prove that there are two points on the curve with equation $y = x^3 - 11x + 1$ at which the tangent is parallel to $y = x$. Find the value of $\dfrac{d^2y}{dx^2}$ at each point.

Test yourself	**What to review**
	If your answer is incorrect:
1 Find the derivative of: $$3x^8 + \frac{4}{x^3}$$	*Review Heinemann Book P1 pages 135–137*
2 Find the derivative of: $$(2x^2 - 3x)\left(x - \frac{4}{x}\right)$$	*Review Heinemann Book P1 pages 135–137*
3 Find the second derivative of: $$(2x^2 - 3x)\left(x - \frac{4}{x}\right)$$	*Review Heinemann Book P1 pages 135–137 and 139–140*
4 Find the set of values of x for which **(a)** f is increasing **(b)** f is decreasing when $f(x) = 2x^3 - 9x^2 + 12x$	*Review Heinemann Book P1 pages 138–139*
5 Find an equation of the tangent and an equation of the normal to the curve with equation $y = 7x^3 - 3x - 2$ at the point $(1, 2)$.	*Review Heinemann Book P1 pages 143–144*
6 Find and distinguish the nature of the turning point on the curve with equation $y = \dfrac{1}{x^2} - 2x$	*Review Heinemann Book P1 pages 140–143*
7 Equal squares of side x cm are removed from each corner of a rectangular sheet measuring 8 cm by 5 cm. The edges are then turned up to make an open box of volume V cm^3. Show that $V = 40x - 26x^2 + 4x^3$. Given that x can vary, find the maximum value of V and the corresponding value of x.	*Review Heinemann Book P1 pages 144–150*

Test yourself answers

1 $24x^7 - \dfrac{12}{x^4}$ **2** $6x^2 - 8 - 6x$ **3** $12x - 6$ **4 (a)** f increasing when $x < 1$ and $x > 2$ **(b)** f decreasing when $1 < x < 2$

5 Tangent: $y - 2 = 18(x - 1)$ Normal: $y - 2 = -\frac{1}{18}(x - 1)$ **6** Minimum at $(-1, 3)$ **7** Maximum value of V is 18 at $x = 1$

Integration

6

Key points to remember

1 $\int k\,dx = kx + C$, where k is a constant.

2 $\int x^n\,dx = \dfrac{1}{n+1}x^{n+1} + C, n \neq -1$

3 $\int (u+v)\,dx = \int u\,dx + \int v\,dx$

4 The differential equation $\dfrac{dy}{dx} = f'(x)$ is a **first order** equation. Its solution is $y = f(x) + C$.

5 The solution of a differential equation that contains one or more arbitrary constants is called the **general solution** of the equation.

6 The conditions which allow you to evaluate the arbitrary constant(s) in the general solution are called the **boundary conditions.**

7 A solution to a differential equation in which the arbitrary constant is known is called a **particular solution.**

8 The definite integral
$$\int_a^b f'(x)\,dx = \Big[f(x)\Big]_a^b = f(b) - f(a)$$
if f' is the derived function of f throughout the interval (a, b).
The numbers a and b are called the **limits of integration.**

9 The area of the region bounded by the curve with equation $y = f(x)$, the ordinates $x = a$ and $x = b$ and the x-axis can be found by evaluating the definite integral
$$\int_a^b f(x)\,dx, \text{ when it exists.}$$

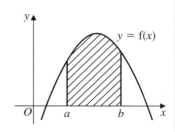

10 The area of the region bounded by the curve with
equation $x = g(y)$, the lines $y = \alpha$ and $y = \beta$ and the
y-axis can be found by evaluating the definite integral

$$\int_\alpha^\beta g(y)\,\mathrm{d}y,\text{ when it exists.}$$

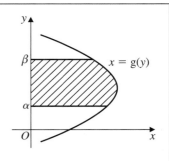

Example 1
Find:

(a) $\displaystyle\int x^8\,\mathrm{d}x$

(b) $\displaystyle\int \frac{4}{x^3}\,\mathrm{d}x$

(c) $\displaystyle\int \left(\sqrt{x} - \frac{3}{x}\right)^2\,\mathrm{d}x$

Answer

(a) $\displaystyle\int x^8\,\mathrm{d}x = \tfrac{1}{9}x^9 + C$ | Using **2** |

(b) $\displaystyle\int \frac{4}{x^3}\,\mathrm{d}x = \int 4x^{-3}\,\mathrm{d}x$ | Using $\dfrac{1}{x^a} = x^{-a}$ |

$$= \frac{4}{-3+1}x^{-3+1} + C$$ | Using **2** |

$$= -\tfrac{4}{2}x^{-2} + C$$

$$= -2x^{-2} + C$$

$$= -\frac{2}{x^2} + C$$

(c) $\displaystyle\int \left(\sqrt{x} - \frac{3}{x}\right)^2\,\mathrm{d}x$

$$= \int \left[(\sqrt{x})^2 + 2(\sqrt{x})\left(-\frac{3}{x}\right) + \left(-\frac{3}{x}\right)^2\right]\mathrm{d}x$$ | Using $(a+b)^2 \equiv a^2 + 2ab + b^2$ |

$$= \int \left(x - \frac{6x^{\frac{1}{2}}}{x} + \frac{9}{x^2}\right)\mathrm{d}x$$

$$= \int \left(x - 6x^{\frac{1}{2}}x^{-1} + 9x^{-2}\right)\mathrm{d}x$$ | Using $\dfrac{1}{x^a} = x^{-a}$ |

$$= \int \left(x - 6x^{-\frac{1}{2}} + 9x^{-2}\right)\mathrm{d}x$$ | Using $x^a \times x^b = x^{a+b}$ |

$$= \tfrac{1}{2}x^2 - \frac{6}{-\frac{1}{2}+1}x^{-\frac{1}{2}+1} + \frac{9}{-2+1}x^{-2+1} + C$$ | Using **2** |

$$= \tfrac{1}{2}x^2 - \frac{6}{\tfrac{1}{2}}x^{\frac{1}{2}} + \frac{9}{-1}x^{-1} + C$$

$$= \tfrac{1}{2}x^2 - 12x^{\frac{1}{2}} - 9x^{-1} + C$$

$$= \tfrac{1}{2}x^2 - 12\sqrt{x} - \frac{9}{x} + C$$

Worked examination question 1

(a) Find the general solution of the differential equation

$$\frac{dy}{dx} = 6x^2 - 8x + 5.$$

(b) Find the particular solution of the equation for which $y = -2$ at $x = 2$.

Answer

(a) $\dfrac{dy}{dx} = 6x^2 - 8x + 5$

So $\qquad y = \displaystyle\int (6x^2 - 8x + 5)\,dx$ 　　　　　　　　 Using **4**

$$y = \frac{6x^3}{3} - \frac{8x^2}{2} + 5x + C$$ 　　　　Using **1** and **2**

$$y = 2x^3 - 4x^2 + 5x + C \text{ is the general solution}$$ 　Using **5**

(b) Using the boundary condition that $y = -2$ at $x = 2$
in $\qquad y = 2x^3 - 4x^2 + 5x + C$

gives $-2 = 2(2^3) - 4(2^2) + 5(2) + C$ 　　　　　Using **6**

$$-2 = 16 - 16 + 10 + C$$

$$-2 = 10 + C$$

$\Rightarrow \qquad C = -12$

So the particular solution is 　　　　　　　　　Using **7**
$\qquad y = 2x^3 - 4x^2 + 5x - 12$

Example 2

Evaluate $\displaystyle\int_1^8 x^{-\frac{1}{3}}\,dx$.

Answer

$$\int_1^8 x^{-\frac{1}{3}}\,dx$$

$$= \left[\frac{1}{\tfrac{2}{3}}x^{\frac{2}{3}}\right]_1^8$$ 　　　　　　　Using **2**

$$= \left[\tfrac{3}{2}x^{\frac{2}{3}}\right]_1^8$$

$$= \tfrac{3}{2} \times 8^{\frac{2}{3}} - \left(\tfrac{3}{2} \times 1^{\frac{2}{3}}\right)$$ 　　　Using **8**

$$= \tfrac{3}{2} \times 2^2 - \left(\tfrac{3}{2} \times 1^2\right)$$ 　　　Since $a^{\frac{2}{3}} = (\sqrt[3]{a})^2$

$$= \left(\tfrac{3}{2} \times 4\right) - \left(\tfrac{3}{2} \times 1\right)$$
$$= 6 - 1\tfrac{1}{2}$$
$$= 4\tfrac{1}{2}$$

Example 3

Find the ratio of the area of region R_1 to the area of region R_2 in the diagram.

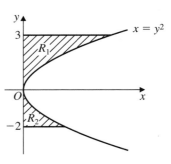

Answer

Area of $R_1 = \displaystyle\int_0^3 x\,\mathrm{d}y$

> Using **10**

$$= \int_0^3 y^2\,\mathrm{d}y$$

> Since $x = y^2$

$$= \left[\tfrac{1}{3}y^3\right]_0^3$$

> Using **2**

$$= \left[\tfrac{1}{3} \times 3^3\right] - \left[\tfrac{1}{3} \times 0^3\right]$$

> Using **8**

$$= 9 - 0 = 9$$

Area of $R_2 = \displaystyle\int_{-2}^0 x\,\mathrm{d}y$

> Using **10**

$$= \int_{-2}^0 y^2\,\mathrm{d}y$$

> Since $x = y^2$

$$= \left[\tfrac{1}{3}y^3\right]_{-2}^0$$

> Using **2**

$$= \left[\tfrac{1}{3} \times 0^3\right] - \left[\tfrac{1}{3} \times (-2)^3\right]$$

> Using **8**

$$= 0 + \tfrac{8}{3} = \tfrac{8}{3}$$

Ratio of $R_1 : R_2 = 9 : \tfrac{8}{3}$
$$= 27 : 8$$

Worked examination question 2

The points $A(1, 2)$ and $B(3, 0)$ lie on the curve with equation $y = x(3 - x)$ as shown in the diagram.
Find the area of the shaded region bounded by the curve and the line AB.

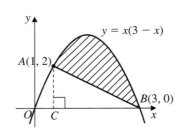

Answer

Let C be the foot of the perpendicular from A to the x-axis. Then C has coordinates $(1, 0)$ so $OC = 1$ and $AC = 2$ and $BC = 3 - 1 = 2$.

Area of $\triangle\ ABC = \frac{1}{2} \times 2 \times 2 = 2$ units^2

Area of region bounded by the curve, the x-axis and the line $x = 1$ is given by

$$\int_1^3 y\,dx$$
Using 9

$$= \int_1^3 x(3 - x)\,dx$$
Since $y = x(3 - x)$

$$= \int_1^3 (3x - x^2)\,dx$$

$$= \left[\frac{3x^2}{2} - \frac{1}{3}x^3\right]_1^3$$
Using 2

Using 8

$$= \left(\tfrac{3}{2} \times 3^2 - \tfrac{1}{3} \times 3^3\right) - \left(\tfrac{3}{2} \times 1^2 - \tfrac{1}{3} \times 1^3\right)$$

$$= \left(\tfrac{27}{2} - 9\right) - \left(\tfrac{3}{2} - \tfrac{1}{3}\right)$$

$$= 4\tfrac{1}{2} - \tfrac{7}{6}$$

$$= 3\tfrac{1}{3} \text{ units}^2$$

So the area of the shaded region is $3\frac{1}{3} - 2 = 1\frac{1}{3}$ units^2.

Revision exercise 6

1 Find these integrals:

(a) $\displaystyle\int \frac{1}{3}x^4\,dx$ **(b)** $\displaystyle\int (2x - 1)(2x + 1)\,dx$ **(c)** $\displaystyle\int (x^{-2} - x^{-3})\,dx$

(d) $\displaystyle\int 2x^{\frac{1}{3}}\,dx$ **(e)** $\displaystyle\int (x - x^{-1})^2\,dx$

2 Evaluate these definite integrals:

(a) $\displaystyle\int_{-2}^2 3x^3\,dx$ **(b)** $\displaystyle\int_1^9 \frac{1}{\sqrt{x}}\,dx$ **(c)** $\displaystyle\int_{\frac{1}{2}}^{1\frac{1}{2}} (3x + 1)^2\,dx$

(d) $\displaystyle\int_{-2}^4 (3x - 2)(2x + 3)\,dx$ **(e)** $\displaystyle\int_1^4 (\sqrt{x} - 1)^3\,dx$

3 A curve is such that $\dfrac{dy}{dx} = g(x)$ and it passes through the point (a, b).

Find the equation of this curve when:

(a) $g(x) \equiv 4x^3 - 2x$, and $a = 2$, $b = 1$

(b) $g(x) \equiv x - x^2 - x^3$, and $a = 2$, $b = -3$

(c) $g(x) \equiv \dfrac{4 - x^3}{x^2}$, and $a = 1$, $b = -2$

(d) $g(x) \equiv (x^2 + 1)\left(\dfrac{1}{x^2} - 1\right)$, and $a = 1$, $b = \frac{2}{3}$.

4 In each of the following find the area of the finite region bounded by the curve with equation $y = f(x)$ and the x-axis.

(a) $f(x) \equiv 2 + x - x^2$

(b) $f(x) \equiv 4(x - 1)(4 - x)$

(c) $f(x) \equiv 10x + x^2$

5 In each of the following find the area of the finite region bounded by the curve with equation $x = g(y)$ and the y-axis.

(a) $g(y) \equiv 4y - y^2$ **(b)** $g(y) \equiv y^2 - 3y + 2$

(c) $g(y) \equiv -2y^2 - 8y - 6$ **(d)** $g(y) \equiv \frac{3}{2} + 4y + 2y^2$

6 Find the area of the finite region bounded by the curve with equation $y = x^2 - 3x$ and the line $y = x - 3$.

7 The curve for which
$$\frac{dy}{dx} = 2x - \sqrt{x}$$
passes through the point $(\frac{1}{4}, 0)$.
Find:

(a) the equation of the curve in the form $y = f(x)$

(b) the value of y when $x = 4$.

8 Find the positive value of k for which:

(a) $\displaystyle\int_1^k (2x + 3)\,dx = 6$

(b) $\displaystyle\int_k^{3k} x^2\,dx = 1872$

9 Prove that the area of the finite region bounded by the curves with equations $y = x^2$ and $y^2 = 8x$ is $2\frac{2}{3}$ units^2.

10 Prove that the area of the finite region bounded by the curves with equations $y = 5x^2 - 7x + 3$ and $y = x(x + 1)$ is $\frac{2}{3}$ units^2.

Test yourself	What to review

If your answer is incorrect:

1 Find:

(a) $\displaystyle\int \frac{3}{x^5}\,dx$

(b) $\displaystyle\int (2x+1)(3x-2)\,dx$

Review Heinemann Book P1 pages 154–157

2 Evaluate:

(a) $\displaystyle\int_{-2}^{3} 4x^2\,dx$

(b) $\displaystyle\int_{2}^{4} \frac{1}{x^3}\,dx$

Review Heinemann Book P1 pages 160–162

3 Solve the differential equation
$$\frac{dy}{dx} = 3x - \frac{8}{x^2}$$
given that $y = 4$ at $x = 1$.

Review Heinemann Book P1 pages 157–159

4 Find the area of the finite region bounded by the curve with equation $y = -x^2 + 6x - 8$ and the x-axis.

Review Heinemann Book P1 pages 162–170

5 Find the area of the finite region bounded by the curve with equation $x = -y^2 - y + 2$ and the y-axis.

Review Heinemann Book P1 pages 162–170

6 Find the value of the positive integer k for which
$$\int_{1}^{k} (x^2 + 2x)\,dx = 65\tfrac{1}{3}$$

Review Heinemann Book P1 pages 160–162

Test yourself answers

1 (a) $-\frac{3}{4x^4}+C$ (b) $2x^3 - \frac{1}{2}x^2 - 2x + C$ **2** (a) $46\frac{2}{3}$ (b) $\frac{3}{32}$ **3** $y = \frac{3}{2}x^2 + \frac{8}{x} - 5\frac{1}{2}$ **4** $1\frac{1}{3}$ units² **5** $4\frac{1}{2}$ units² **6** $k=5$

Proof

Key points to remember

1 A direct proof has a well defined starting point, followed by a series of valid, logical steps which lead to the required conclusion.

2 $P \Rightarrow Q$ means that P implies Q

3 $P \Leftarrow Q$ means that P is implied by Q

4 $P \Leftrightarrow Q$ means that P is equivalent to Q, or P is a necessary and sufficient condition for Q.

Example 1
Given that $x^2 + y^2 = 2xy$, prove that $x = y$.
Determine whether or not the converse is true.

Answer

$$x^2 + y^2 = 2xy$$
$$\Rightarrow \quad x^2 - 2xy + y^2 = 0$$
$$\Rightarrow \quad (x - y)^2 = 0$$
$$\Rightarrow \quad x - y = 0 \Rightarrow x = y$$
Also
$$x = y$$
$$\Rightarrow \quad x - y = 0$$
$$\Rightarrow \quad (x - y)^2 = 0$$
$$\Rightarrow \quad x^2 - 2xy + y^2 = 0$$
$$\Rightarrow \quad x^2 + y^2 = 2xy$$

So the converse is true, i.e. $x^2 + y^2 = 2xy \Leftrightarrow x = y$

Example 2
The angle θ is positive and less than $180°$. Given that $\theta = 45°$, prove that $\sin^2 \theta = \frac{1}{2}$.

Prove also that the converse is **not** true.

Answer

In the diagram, the triangle is isosceles and right-angled so each of the acute angles are of size 45°. If the two equal sides are each of length 1, then by Pythagoras the hypotenuse is $\sqrt{2}$.

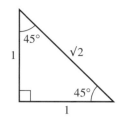

So
$$\sin 45° = \frac{1}{\sqrt{2}}$$

$\Rightarrow \qquad\qquad \sin^2 45° = \tfrac{1}{2}$

So if $\theta = 45°$, then $\sin^2 \theta = \tfrac{1}{2}$

For the converse,

if $\qquad \sin^2 \theta = \tfrac{1}{2}$

then $\qquad \sin \theta = \pm\dfrac{1}{\sqrt{2}}$

If $\sin \theta = +\tfrac{1}{2}$ then θ lies in the 1st or 2nd quadrant so $\theta = 45°$ **or** 135°. Consequently the converse is not true:

i.e. $\sin \theta = 45° \Rightarrow \sin^2 \theta = \dfrac{1}{\sqrt{2}}$

But $\sin^2 \theta = \dfrac{1}{\sqrt{2}} \not\Rightarrow \sin \theta = 45°$

Revision exercise 7

1 All the terms of a particular geometric series are positive. The first term is p and the second term is $p^2 - p$.
Prove that this series is convergent if $1 < p < 2$.

2 The first, second and nth terms of an arithmetic series are a, b and l.
Prove that the sum of all n terms in this series is:
$$\frac{(a+l)(b+l-2a)}{2(b-a)}.$$

3 Prove that:
$$(1 + \sin x + \cos x)^2 \Leftrightarrow 2(1 + \sin x)(1 + \cos x)$$
for all values of x.

4 Given that
$$16\cos^2 \theta + 3\sin^2 \theta = 7$$
prove that $4\tan^2 \theta = 9$.
Investigate whether or not the converse is true.

5 If m is an integer, explain why $2m + 1$ is an odd integer.
Prove that if n is an integer, the next odd integer is
$$n + 1 + \sin^2\left(\frac{n\pi}{2}\right).$$

6 The tangent at $A(1, -3)$ to the curve with equation
$y = x^3 - x^2 - 4x + 1$ meets the curve again at B.
Prove that:
(a) the tangent passes through the origin O
(b) B has coordinates $(-1, 3)$.

7 Prove that the points $(3, -5)$, $(4, 1)$ and $(6, 13)$ lie on the
same line.
Find the coordinates of the points where this line meets the
coordinate axes.

8 Prove that the points $(3, -5)$, $(-1, 3)$ and $(11, 9)$ are the
vertices of a right-angled triangle and find the area of
this triangle.

9 Given that $6 \sin^2 \theta = 5 + \cos \theta$, prove that **either** $\cos \theta = \frac{1}{3}$ **or**
$\cos \theta = -\frac{1}{2}$.

10 The angle θ lies between 0 and 2π radians and $\sin 2\theta = \sin \frac{\pi}{6}$.
Prove that $\theta = \frac{13\pi}{12}$ and three other values, each of which is to
be found in terms of π.

Test yourself	What to review
	If your answers are incorrect:
1 Given that $a = x + \frac{1}{x}$ and $b = x - \frac{1}{x}$, prove that $b^2 = a^2 - 4$.	*Review Heinemann Book P1 pages 173–176*
2 Given that the rth term of a series is u_r, where $u_r = 2r - 1$, prove that $u_{2r} = 2u_r + 1$	*Review Heinemann Book P1 pages 173–176*
3 Given that $f(n) = \frac{1}{n(n+1)}$, prove that $f(n) - f(n+1) = \frac{2}{n(n+1)(n+2)}$	*Review Heinemann Book P1 pages 173–176*

Test yourself answers

1    $b = x - \dfrac{1}{x}$

$\Rightarrow \quad b^2 = \left(x - \dfrac{1}{x}\right)^2$

$\Rightarrow \quad b^2 = x^2 + 2x\left(-\dfrac{1}{x}\right) + \left(-\dfrac{1}{x}\right)^2$ | Using $(x + y)^2 \equiv x^2 + 2xy + y^2$ |

$\qquad = x^2 - 2 + \dfrac{1}{x^2}$

$\qquad = x^2 + 2 + \dfrac{1}{x^2} - 4$

$\qquad = \left(x + \dfrac{1}{x}\right)^2 - 4$ | Using $x^2 + 2xy + y^2 \equiv (x + y)^2$ |

$\qquad b^2 = a^2 - 4$

2    $u_r = 2r - 1$
So $u_{2r} = 2(2r) - 1$
$\qquad\quad = 4r - 1$
$\qquad\quad = 4r - 2 + 1$
$\qquad\quad = 2(2r - 1) + 1$
So $u_{2r} = 2u_r + 1$

3    $f(n) = \dfrac{1}{n(n + 1)}$

So $f(n + 1) = \dfrac{1}{[n + 1][(n + 1) + 1]}$

$\qquad\qquad = \dfrac{1}{(n + 1)(n + 2)}$

Hence $f(n) - f(n + 1)$

$\qquad = \dfrac{1}{n(n + 1)} - \dfrac{1}{(n + 1)(n + 2)}$

$\qquad = \dfrac{(n + 2) - n}{n(n + 1)(n + 2)}$

$\qquad = \dfrac{n + 2 - n}{n(n + 1)(n + 2)}$

$\qquad = \dfrac{2}{n(n + 1)(n + 2)}$

Examination style paper

Attempt **all** questions.   **Time 90 minutes**

1   Figure 1 shows two concentric circular sectors centre O, radius 5 cm
    and 7 cm respectively, subtending an angle of 2.6^c at O.
    For the shaded region, find:
    (a) the perimeter   **(2 marks)**
    (b) the area.   **(3 marks)**

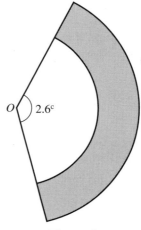

Figure 1

2   A certain geometric series has first term 60 and common ratio 1.002.
    Find:
    (a) the 100th term of the series, giving your answer to 2 decimal
    places   **(3 marks)**
    (b) the sum of the first 100 terms of the series, giving your answer
    to the nearest integer.   **(4 marks)**

3   Given that
    $$f(x) \equiv \frac{(x^{\frac{1}{2}} + 1)^2}{x^{\frac{1}{2}}}, \qquad x > 0$$
    (a) prove that $f(x) \equiv x^{\frac{1}{2}} + 2 + x^{-\frac{1}{2}}$ **(2 marks)**

    (b) evaluate $\displaystyle\int_1^4 f(x)\,dx$.   **(5 marks)**

4   (a) By considering sketch graphs of the curves with equations
    $y = \sin x$ and $y = \sin 2x$, or otherwise, find for $0 \leqslant x \leqslant 360°$, the
    values of x, in degrees, for which:
    $$\sin x = \sin 2x.$$ **(5 marks)**
    (b) Find, in radians to 2 decimal places, the values of t for which:
    $$\tan t = -7 \text{ and } -\pi < t < 3\pi.$$ **(5 marks)**

5   Figure 2 shows the line OA with equation $y = x(\sqrt{2} - 1)$. The x-coordinate of A is 3 and the line AB is perpendicular to OA and meets the x-axis at B.

(a) Find the value of α, where $\alpha = \angle AOB$.   **(2 marks)**
(b) Show that the gradient of AB is $-(\sqrt{2} + 1)$.   **(3 marks)**
(c) Determine the area of $\triangle\ AOB$, giving your answer in the form $(m + n\sqrt{2})$, where m and n are numbers to be found.

                                                        (5 marks)

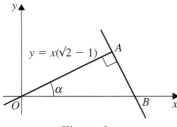

Figure 2

6   Figure 3 shows part of the curve with equation $y = 4 - x^2$ and the tangent to the curve at $A(1, 3)$ which meets the x-axis at B.
The region P is bounded by the curve, Ox and Oy and the region Q is bounded by the curve, the tangent and the x-axis, as shown.

(a) Prove that $OB = 2.5$ units of length.   **(4 marks)**
(b) Find the area of region P.   **(3 marks)**
(c) Find the area of region Q.   **(5 marks)**

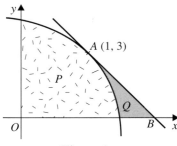

Figure 3

7   A solid right circular cylinder, base radius x cm and height h cm, has a fixed volume of $1000\ \text{cm}^3$.

(a) Express h in terms of x.   **(2 marks)**

The total surface area of the cylinder is $A\ \text{cm}^2$.

(b) Prove that $A = 2\pi x^2 + \dfrac{2000}{x}$.   **(2 marks)**

(c) Given that x varies, prove that A takes a stationary value when $x^3 = \dfrac{500}{\pi}$.   **(4 marks)**

(d) Prove that this stationary value of A is a minimum and determine its value to 1 decimal place.   **(4 marks)**

8   Figure 4 shows a sketch of the curve with equation $y = x^2 - x + 1$ which cuts the y-axis at A. The stationary point on the curve is B.

(a) Find the coordinates of A and B.   **(4 marks)**
(b) Explain why the equation $x^2 - x + 1 = 0$ has no real roots.

                                                        (1 mark)
(c) Divide $x^3 + 1$ by $x^2 - x + 1$.   **(2 marks)**
(d) Hence, or otherwise, find the set of values of k for which the equation:

$$x^3 + 1 = kx + k$$

has three real roots.   **(5 marks)**

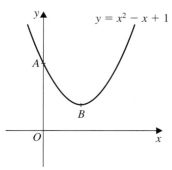

Figure 4

Answers

Revision exercise 1

1 25

2 $14\sqrt{5}$

4 (a) 1.08, −2.08   (b) $\frac{49}{4}$

5 (a) $\frac{1}{2}(2 + 3\sqrt{6})\,\text{cm}^2$ (b) 5 cm

6 (b) least value 2 when $y = 0$

7 $x + y = \pm 5$, $x - y = \sqrt{21}$

8 $(4x + 1)(x + 7)$; 401, 107

9 (a) $2(x + 1)^2$ (b) $5x(x + 2)$

10 (a) $x < 1$ (b) $-4 < x < \frac{2}{3}$

11 (a) $\left(\frac{4}{3}, \frac{2}{3}\right)$, $\left(-\frac{4}{3}, -\frac{2}{3}\right)$ (b) $(4, 3)$, $\left(-\frac{3}{5}, -20\right)$

12 $m = -9$, $n = -\frac{2}{3}$

13 (a) $2^{\frac{2}{3}} - 1$

14 $a = \frac{2}{3}$, $b = \frac{1}{3}$

15 $A = 11 + 5\sqrt{5}$, $B = 2 + \sqrt{5}$

16 $\pm(\sqrt{6} + \sqrt{5})$

17 1.63, −1.23

18 $(1, -1)$, $\left(-\frac{3}{13}, \frac{11}{13}\right)$

19 $p = -14$, $q = 48$; third factor is $(x - 8)$

20 (a) $(3, 7)$, $(27, 47)$

     (b) 0.6

21 (a) (i) $\frac{1}{5}$ (ii) $\frac{24}{25}$

     (b) $x = 2$, $y = 1$

Revision exercise 2

4 (a) −0.993, −8.14   (b) −0.574, 0.819

     (c) −0.401, 2.29   (d) −0.497, −0.573

     (e) −0.751, 0.660

5 (a) 243.1°   (b) 82.7°   (c) 10.2°

     (d) 50.8°   (e) 108.4°

6 (a) 0.61, 2.54   (b) 2.08, 4.20

     (c) 0.66, 2.48, 3.81, 5.62

7 (a) −150°, −30°, 210°, 330°, 570°, 690°

     (b) −150°, 30°, 210°, 390°, 570°

9 (a) $\frac{12}{13}$, $-\frac{5}{13}$ (b) $-\frac{35}{37}$, $-\frac{35}{12}$

     (c) $-\frac{15}{17}$, $-\frac{8}{15}$

10 1.32, 4.97

11 1.23, 3.14, 5.05

12 (a) (i) 39 cm   (ii) 95 cm²

     (b) $16\pi\,\text{cm}^2$

13 (a) 2.5   (b) 27 : 29

14 (a) 20.9 cm   (b) 31.5 cm²

Revision exercise 3

1 (a) $2x + 5y + 8 = 0$ (b) $4x + 9y = 5$

     (c) $y = 4x - 5$ (d) $y - x = 7$

2 (b) $(2, 3)$

3 (a) $y = 2x + 3$ (b) $(1, 5)$

     (c) 13 units

4 (b) 60 units²   (c) $(1, 15)$

5 (a) $3y - x = 0$ (b) $y + x = 0$

     (c) $x - y = 6$

6 $q = -\frac{3}{22}$

7 $5x - 3y - 3 = 0$

8 (a) $\left(4, \frac{3}{2}\right)$, $\left(\frac{9}{5}, -\frac{9}{5}\right)$ (b) $60y + 40x = 107$

9 (a) $2y - 3x = 0$ (b) 1.302 units

Revision exercise 4

1 (a) $u_{50} = -69.9$, $S_{50} = -1535$

     (b) $u_2 = 11$, $u_{16} = 53$

     (c) $n = 42$, $S_{42} = 2877$

     (d) $u_1 = 6$, $n = 40$

2 (a) $v_{15} = 4.40$, $S_{15} = 482$

     (b) $v_{10} = -15.4$, $S_{10} = -9.07$

     (c) $n = 9$, $S_9 = -21.4$

     (d) $n = 6$, $v_n = 9.72$

3 $\frac{2}{3}$

4 $20\frac{5}{6}$, $111\frac{5}{6}$

5 First term 40, common difference −2; $n = 42$

6 $m = 2$, $n = 4$

7 44 550

8 $-853\frac{1}{3}$

9   **(a)** $5, \frac{1}{3}$ **(b)** 11 terms

10 **(a)** $\sqrt{2}, 4\sqrt{6}$ **(b)** 225

     (c) 50

Revision exercise 5

1   **(a)** $3x^2 - 4$ **(b)** $15x^4 - 15x^2$

    (c) $4x + \dfrac{3}{x^2}$

2   **(a)** $x^{-\frac{1}{2}} - 2x^{-\frac{1}{3}}$

    (b) $\frac{3}{2}\left(x^{\frac{1}{2}} - x^{-\frac{1}{2}} - x^{-\frac{3}{2}} + x^{-\frac{5}{2}}\right)$

    (c) $2x + \dfrac{2}{x^3}$

3   Tangents are $y - 1 = 3(x - 2)$ and
$y + 1 = x - 1$.
Normals are $y - 1 = -\frac{1}{3}(x - 2)$ and
$y + 1 = -1(x - 1)$.

4 $y = -\frac{1}{8}x + 4\frac{1}{4}$

5   **(a)** (i) $x > 5$ or $x < -5$

       (ii) $-5 < x < 5$

    (b) (i) $-1 < x < 0$

       (ii) $x > 0$ or $x < -1$

    (c) (i) $x < -2, 0 < x < 2$

       (ii) $-2 < x < 0, x > 2$

6   **(a)** $(3, -54)$ min, $(-3, 54)$ max

    (b) $(0, 0)$ min, $(\frac{1}{3}, \frac{1}{27})$ max

    (c) $(2, \frac{1}{6})$ min, $(-2, -\frac{1}{6})$ max

7 $\frac{32}{27}\pi \, \mathrm{m}^3$

8   **(a)** $8, -10$ **(b)** $a = \frac{8}{3}, b = \frac{5}{6}$

9   12 and -12

Revision exercise 6

1   **(a)** $\frac{1}{15}x^5 + C$ **(b)** $\frac{4}{3}x^3 - x + C$

    (c) $\frac{1}{2}x^{-2} - x^{-1} + C$ **(d)** $\frac{3}{2}x^{\frac{4}{3}} + C$

    (e) $\frac{1}{3}x^3 - 2x - x^{-1} + C$

2   **(a)** 0   **(b)** 4   **(c)** $16\frac{3}{4}$

    (d) 138   **(e)** $\frac{9}{10}$

3   **(a)** $y = x^4 - x^2 - 11$

    (b) $y = \dfrac{x^2}{2} - \dfrac{x^3}{3} - \dfrac{x^4}{4} + \dfrac{5}{3}$

    (c) $y = \dfrac{5}{2} - \dfrac{4}{x} - \dfrac{x^2}{2}$

    (d) $y = 2 - x^{-1} - \dfrac{x^3}{3}$

4   **(a)** $4\frac{1}{2}$ **(b)** 18

    (c) $\frac{500}{3}$

5   **(a)** $\frac{32}{3}$ **(b)** $\frac{1}{6}$

    (c) $\frac{8}{3}$ **(d)** $\frac{1}{3}$

6 $\frac{4}{3}$

7   **(a)** $y = x^2 - \frac{2}{3}x^{\frac{3}{2}} + \frac{1}{48}$

    (b) $10\frac{11}{16}$

8   **(a)** 2   **(b)** 6

Revision exercise 7

4   The converse is true.

7 $(\frac{23}{6}, 0), (0, -23)$

8   60 units^2

10 $\frac{\pi}{12}, \frac{5\pi}{12}, \frac{17\pi}{12}$

Answers to examination style paper

1   **(a)** 35.2 cm   **(b)** 31.2 cm^2

2   **(a)** 73.12   **(b)** 6635

3   **(b)** $12\frac{2}{3}$

4   **(a)** 0, 60°, 180°, 300°, 360°

    (b) $-1.43, 1.71, 4.85, 8.00$

5   **(a)** 22.5°   **(c)** $(27\sqrt{2} - 36)$ units^2

6   **(b)** $\frac{16}{3}$ units^2 **(c)** $\frac{7}{12}$ units^2

7   **(a)** $h = \dfrac{1000}{\pi x^2}$ **(d)** 553.6

8   **(a)** $A(0, 1), B(\frac{1}{2}, \frac{3}{4})$

    (c) $x + 1$

    (d) $k > \frac{3}{4}$